# SOLOING**SECRETS** OF**THE**GUITAR**GODS**

Get Inside the Techniques & Styles of the Greatest Rock Guitarists Ever

EDITED BY JASON**SHADRICK** & ANDY**ELLIS**

**PREMIERGuitar**

FUNDAMENTAL**CHANGES**

# Soloing Secrets of the Guitar Gods

## Get Inside the Techniques & Styles of the Greatest Rock Guitarists Ever

ISBN: 978-1-78933-089-2

Published by **www.fundamental-changes.com**

Copyright © 2019 Gearhead Communications

**premierguitar.com**

Over 700,000 fans on Facebook: **facebook.com/premierguitar**

Instagram: **instagram.com/premierguitar**

YouTube: **youtube.com/premierguitar**

For over 500 free guitar lessons check out

**premierguitar.com/lessons**

Cover Image Copyright: Dimitrius/Adobe Stock Photos

# Contents

# Introduction

One of the most important musical lessons of my life happened in grad school during a clinic with the legendary jazz trumpeter Clark Terry. In the middle of the clinic, he explained that the entire process of learning jazz can be summed up in three words: Imitate. Assimilate. Innovate. Though they might be easy to remember, it can take a lifetime to truly understand these words and put them into practice. This book is designed to help put you on that path.

When learning any new language—musical or otherwise—it's common practice to mimic those who came before you. For guitarists, imitation can be as simple as learning the chords to a Taylor Swift song or as challenging as mapping out a demanding Guthrie Govan tapping lick. The first step is to get those sounds under your fingers. Your execution doesn't have to be perfect or at full tempo. You don't even have to get the notes exactly right. Just start somewhere and move forward—that's the secret.

Assimilation is simply a fancy word for deeply understanding or internalizing a concept or musical idea. To this day, my wife, who isn't a guitarist, can sing the head from Pat Martino's recording of "Just Friends" simply because I played it over and over in our small college apartment. She had internalized my imitation of Martino's playing to the point where she knew it by heart. Once the raw information is under your fingers and off the page (or recording), then the music begins to pour out. There are many ways to reach this point: You can dissect every note in a solo, work through a tune's harmony, practice a phrase's rhythm and articulation—anything goes. It's at this step that you start to shape your heroes' musical ideas into your own.

Finally, we get to Mr. Terry's last (and most difficult) step: Innovation. The truth is, not everything you learn will carry you this far, but it should always be the goal. True innovation is rare, yet pursuing it will push your playing to levels you probably didn't know existed. A young Eddie Van Halen was so inspired by Eric Clapton's electric blues that he morphed Slowhand's rootsy sounds past the point of recognition, revealing radical new techniques along the way. But innovation doesn't have to be this dramatic. Whenever you discover fresh and inspiring ways to use familiar sounds, you're innovating.

This book presents a collection of original etudes based on the styles of some of today's most revered electric guitarists. Each chapter examines a player's unique sound, style, and technique, while detailing the concepts *and* essential equipment behind the music. Here's an important tip: Unlike a method book, this one doesn't have a beginning, middle, and end. Open it up to any chapter, see if you can isolate a specific passage, and then run with it. Make exercises, riffs, or even entirely new songs out of what you learn. The authors represented here have cracked open the door of inspiration ... now it's time for you to walk through it and explore the world that awaits. —Jason Shadrick

# Get the Audio

The audio files for this book are available to download for free from **premierguitar.com/audio-clips**

We recommend that you download the files directly to your computer, not to your tablet, and extract them there before adding them to your media library. You can then put them on your tablet, iPod, or burn them to CD. If you have any questions head over to **premierguitar.com/contact** and we'll get right back to you.

**premierguitar.com**

Over 700,000 fans on Facebook: **facebook.com/premierguitar**

Instagram: **instagram.com/premierguitar**

YouTube: **youtube.com/premierguitar**

For over 500 free guitar lessons check out **premierguitar.com/lessons**

# Chapter 1: Eric Clapton's "Cream" Years

## By Jamie Humphries

To kick things off, let's look at the legendary Eric Clapton and focus on his early playing—that mid-to-late-'60s period with John Mayall's Bluesbreakers and Cream. It was during this time that "Clapton is God!" graffiti famously appeared in London.

When arranging this study piece, I had three tracks in mind: "Sunshine of Your Love," "Crossroads," and "Badge." The structure of the track is a I–IV–V blues progression in the key of A, although we have a slight twist at the end of our second verse, leading into the solo. Check out the transcription and companion audio.

We begin with a blues riff that outlines A7, the I chord. This section is based around a single-note line on the 4th string enhanced by some double-stops performed on the 4th and 3rd strings. Notice the fast hammer-on that appears on the "and" of beat 4 in the first, third, and seventh measures. This major/minor rub is very common in blues, and it's a great way to create tension and release. This section also includes a climbing, syncopated line that gives the riff a "Sunshine of Your Love"-inspired feel. Pay attention to the rests and cut off the notes to keep things clean and tight.

In measure five, the progression moves to an arpeggiated open-position D7 (IV), followed by our climbing, syncopated riff that has been transposed up a fourth.

The intro riff returns over the next few measures before E7, the V chord, comes in with another major/minor hammer-on. This leads to a short lick based around the E blues scale (E–G–A–Bb–B–D). We then head back to the IV chord with our syncopated, ascending line.

The first chorus concludes with a short blues phrase based around the A minor pentatonic scale (A–C–D–E–G), but again we include both the major and minor 3, which adds slight tension and release to the phrase. Notice how the final two measures are marked with first ending and repeat symbols ... these take us back to the beginning. We repeat the entire verse again, but the final two measures of our rhythm part are slightly different and therefore marked with the second ending.

The second ending introduces another classic EC approach to rhythm playing and includes chord arpeggios based on the parts in "Badge" and "White Room." In the audio track, you'll hear I've included a rotary effect for this section, but we'll get to that in a moment.

Now it's time for our solo, and we dive straight into some bluesy licks based around the A major pentatonic scale (A–B–C#–E–F#). The next two measures include some fast minor-pentatonic lines that include both regular bends and pre-bends, so pay attention to pitch. I should also point out EC's vibrato technique was very fast with a unique approach. Clapton removes his thumb from the back of the neck to achieve his vibrato, and this allows a very free up and down motion on the string that produces a fast and exaggerated sound. Watch the vibrato markings, as they are vital to this section's phrasing.

Notice how we revisit the solo's opening phrase over the IV chord, except this time we pre-bend to C natural, targeting the b7 of D7. We shift up a position in the next measure and perform a large minor-third bend before descending through the A blues scale (A–C–D–Eb–E–G) to conclude with some classic blues licks.

The next few measures make use of a lick similar to Freddie King's "Hide Away." We start off in A major pentatonic, and then shift up a minor third and repeat the lick in A minor pentatonic. The solo ends with a higher position blues-based figure.

**Recording details.** Your tone plays a huge part in how authentic this piece will sound. During this period, Clapton played Gibson SGs and Les Pauls through a 100-watt Marshall. He'd often select the neck pickup and roll back the tone control to achieve a warm, singing sound that became known as the "woman tone."

To emulate EC's tone for this track, I used a Music Man Axis Super Sport loaded with DiMarzio 36th Anniversary PAF pickups. For the bright, clean sounds, I plugged into a Blackstar Series One 50 head with the gain fully up. This gave me a crisp class A sound with the amp breaking up the harder I played. For pedals, I used a Wampler Plexi-Drive, which yielded rich, vintage Marshall sounds.

For the verse, I used the neck pickup with the amp gain rolled off very slightly and a mild overdrive setting. During the "Badge"-style chord arpeggios, I switched to the bridge pickup and backed off the guitar volume slightly so the sound was glassy and brittle. I also added a rotary effect to imitate a Leslie speaker. (If you don't have a rotary effect, try using a chorus or phaser pedal.)

For the solo, I engaged both the bridge and neck humbuckers and rolled off the tone, and also pushed the gain a little harder on the pedal.

Okay—there you have it. There's a lot to get through here, so take your time. And don't stop at playing the correct notes. Really pay attention to dynamics and vibrato, and remember to experiment with your guitar's volume and tone controls.

## Example 1

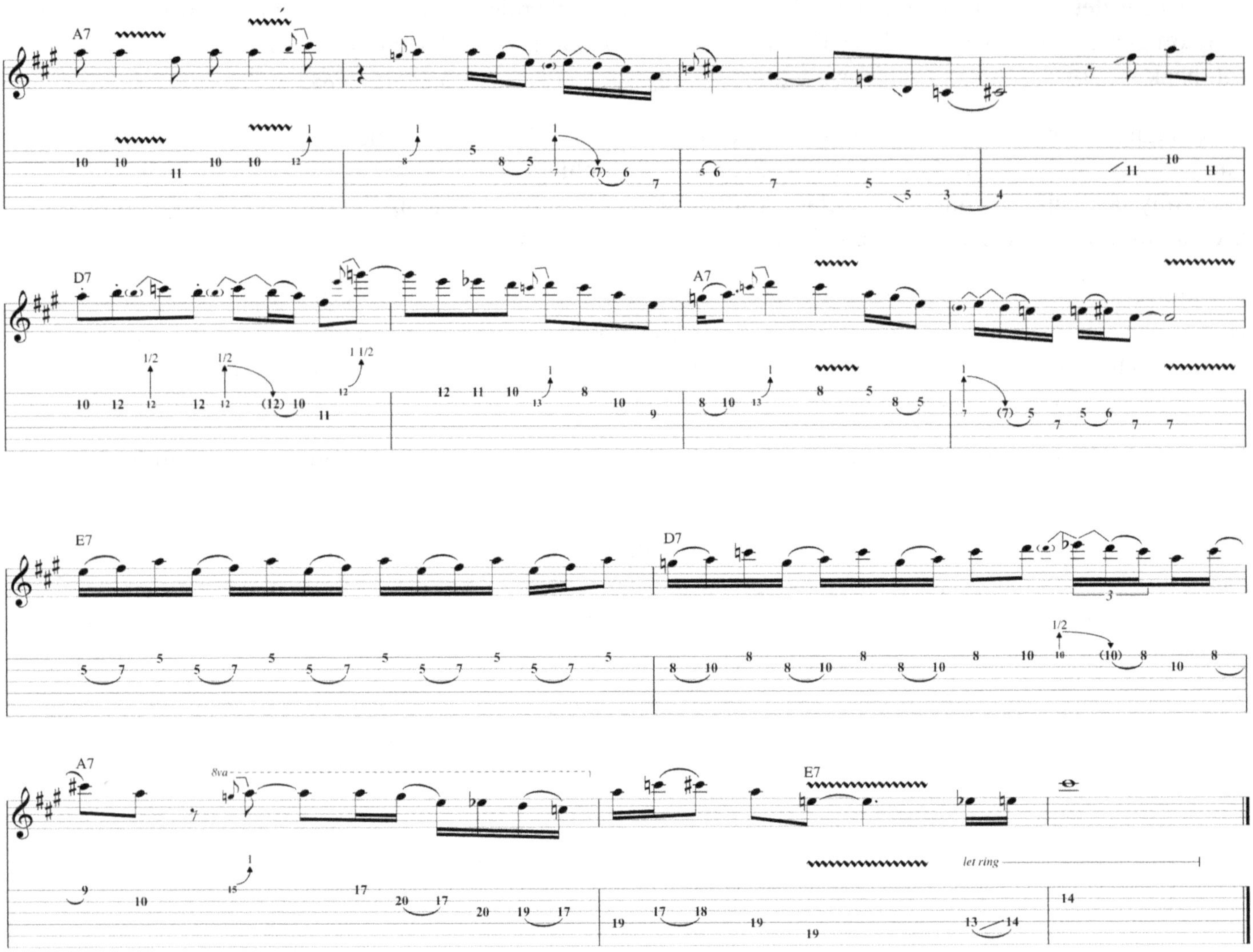
A7
D7
A7
E7
D7
A7
8va
E7
let ring

# Chapter 2: Andy Summers

**By Jamie Humphries**

In this chapter, we explore the style of English guitarist Andy Summers. Like King's X's Ty Tabor, who we'll look at in chapter 12, Summers is a guitarist who flourishes in a trio. The Police were one of the biggest bands to emerge from the late '70s British new wave scene. They reached a global frenzy of success during the '80s with huge tours and unprecedented album sales.

After a brief spell living and working in the United States, Summers relocated to his homeland and met Sting and drummer Stewart Copeland. Sting and Copeland had already formed the Police but invited Summers to join as the fourth member. Originally, the group also featured guitarist Henry Padovani. It wasn't long before Padovani was asked to leave and the classic lineup was born.

The Police achieved mainstream success with a string of five incredibly inventive and influential studio albums, including *Synchronicity*, which went to No. 1 in both the U.S. and U.K. These albums spawned a string of hits, including "Roxanne," "Can't Stand Losing You," "Message in a Bottle," and "Every Breath You Take."

The members of the Police had a volatile relationship, which ultimately led to their breakup. Each member embarked on a solo career: Sting saw the biggest mainstream success, but Copeland and Summers both enjoyed fruitful solo careers. In 2007, the group reformed for a world tour to celebrate their 30th anniversary.

Much like U2's The Edge, Summers has a unique and distinctive style, and he's known mostly for his rhythm technique and use of effects. His playing in the Police featured incredibly tight, syncopated rhythm parts that combined reggae and new wave elements. Summers' jazz background also appeared in his use of more advanced chord shapes and extensions, as well as piano-inspired voicings. When playing leads with the band, Summers mixed subtle, melodic phrases with fast, aggressive pentatonic-based flurries.

The lesson track kicks off with a quintessential rhythm part played on the top three strings. Notice that the Am and Fmaj7 are played the same way, but function differently due to the change in the bass note. This section can be tricky to perform because it requires a very precise sense of rhythm. Make sure you sit back slightly on the beat and don't rush ahead.

We pay tribute to "Walking on the Moon" in the second ending of the first section. The A7sus4 is a signature "Summers" chord. Play it with a healthy dose of echo set to a quarter-note triplet repeat.

The chorus illustrates how new wave and punk influenced Summers' playing. Check out how the simple root-position power chords shift to first-inversion dyads by simply moving the lower note down a half-step. Also, don't overlook the anticipations at the end of every other measure.

The next section uses a mixture of wide-voiced chord shapes (usually a power chord with an added 9), and its influence will be completely obvious to Police fans. Don't panic if your hands aren't quite big enough for these stretches. Summers would simply apply the fingers when needed instead of holding down a chord shape. You'll also notice that we often slide up a half-step to complete the chord, so make sure the slide is clean and clear.

We return to the A7sus4 before launching into some Lenny Breau-style harp harmonics. (Summers used this technique in "Walking on the Moon" and "Regatta de Blanc.") First, hold down an easy Am11 chord by placing your first finger across the top five strings at the 12th fret, and then fretting a C (2nd string, 13th fret) with your second finger. Using your picking-hand index finger, lightly touch the 2nd string 12 frets higher, while plucking it with your middle finger.

In this example, notice how we're alternating fretted notes with harmonics to create a cool, shimmering sound. Once again, use plenty of analog echo.

The track concludes with a short and simple solo, which is based mostly on the A minor pentatonic scale (A–C–D–E–G) and the A Aeolian mode (A–B–C–D–E–F–G). After a bluesy bend, we head into a syncopated descending line before a quick shift down to 3rd position for a fast, legato lick. I copped a few of Summers' jazz-inspired licks for the end of the solo. In the penultimate measure, a short diminished arpeggio outlines the dominant chord (E7) before releasing the tension with the final note.

During the Police era, Summers' main axe was a worn Fender Telecaster that featured a bridge single-coil and a humbucker in the neck position. Usually he plugged the Tele into a Marshall amp for dirty tones and a Roland JC-120 for cleans. Summers would use an Electro-Harmonix flanger for his modulation effects and an old Echoplex for the delay sounds. Pete Cornish built Summers' original rig, but effects guru Bob Bradshaw made his rig for the reunion tour.

**Recording details.** I cut and mixed this entire track on my iPad, due to my touring schedule. I used Steinberg's Cubasis as my DAW, and all of the guitar tones came from Positive Grid's JamUp Pro via an Apogee Jam interface. I used a Marshall-style model with effects based on the EHX Electric Mistress, MXR Dyna Comp, and Echoplex. For the lead tones, I added a Fuzz Face-style effect to the Marshall. As always, I played my trusty Music Man Axis Super Sport, switching between a single-coil setting for rhythm and humbucker mode for extra bite.

**Example 2**

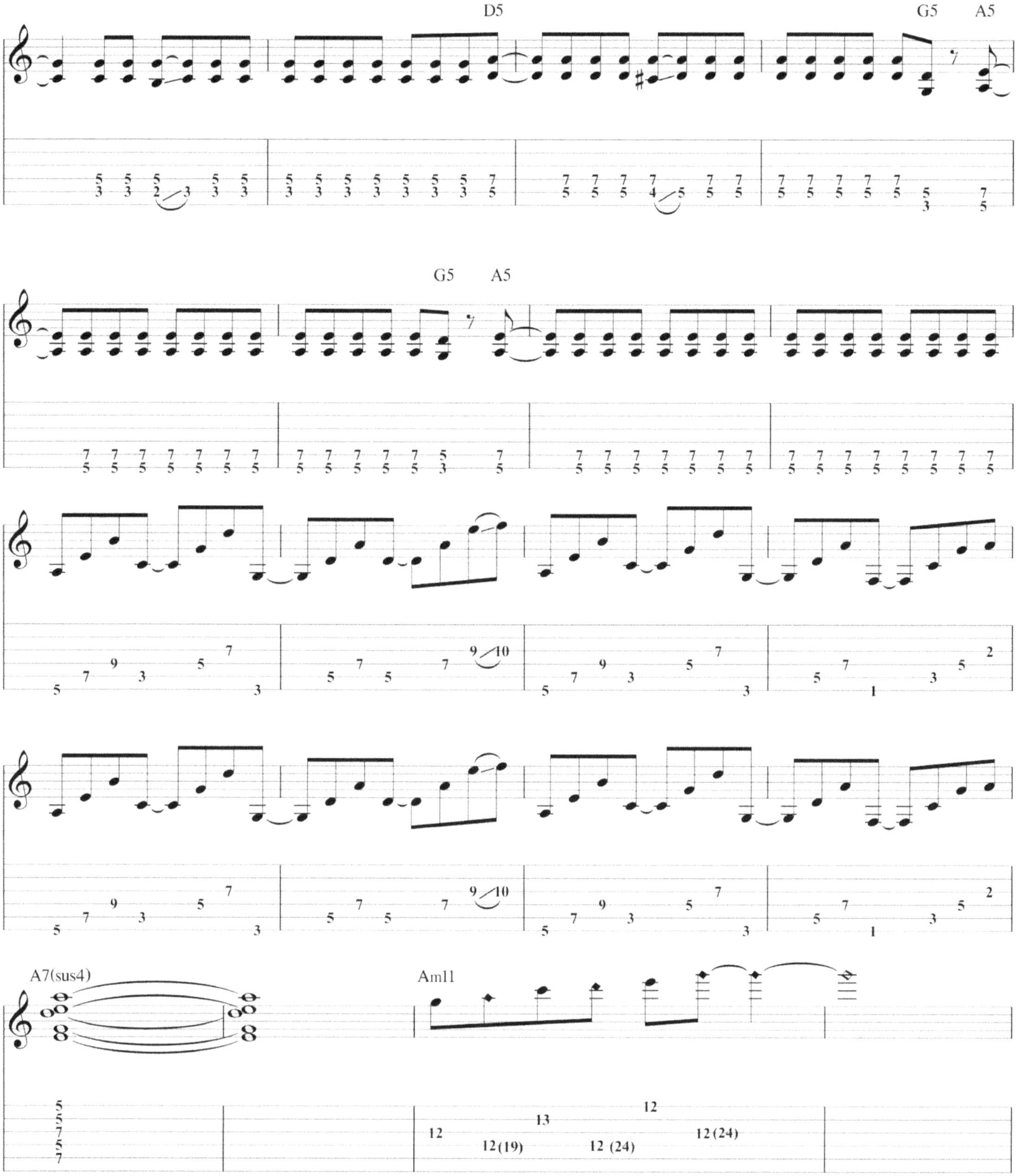
D5
G5
A5
G5
A5
A7(sus4)
Am11

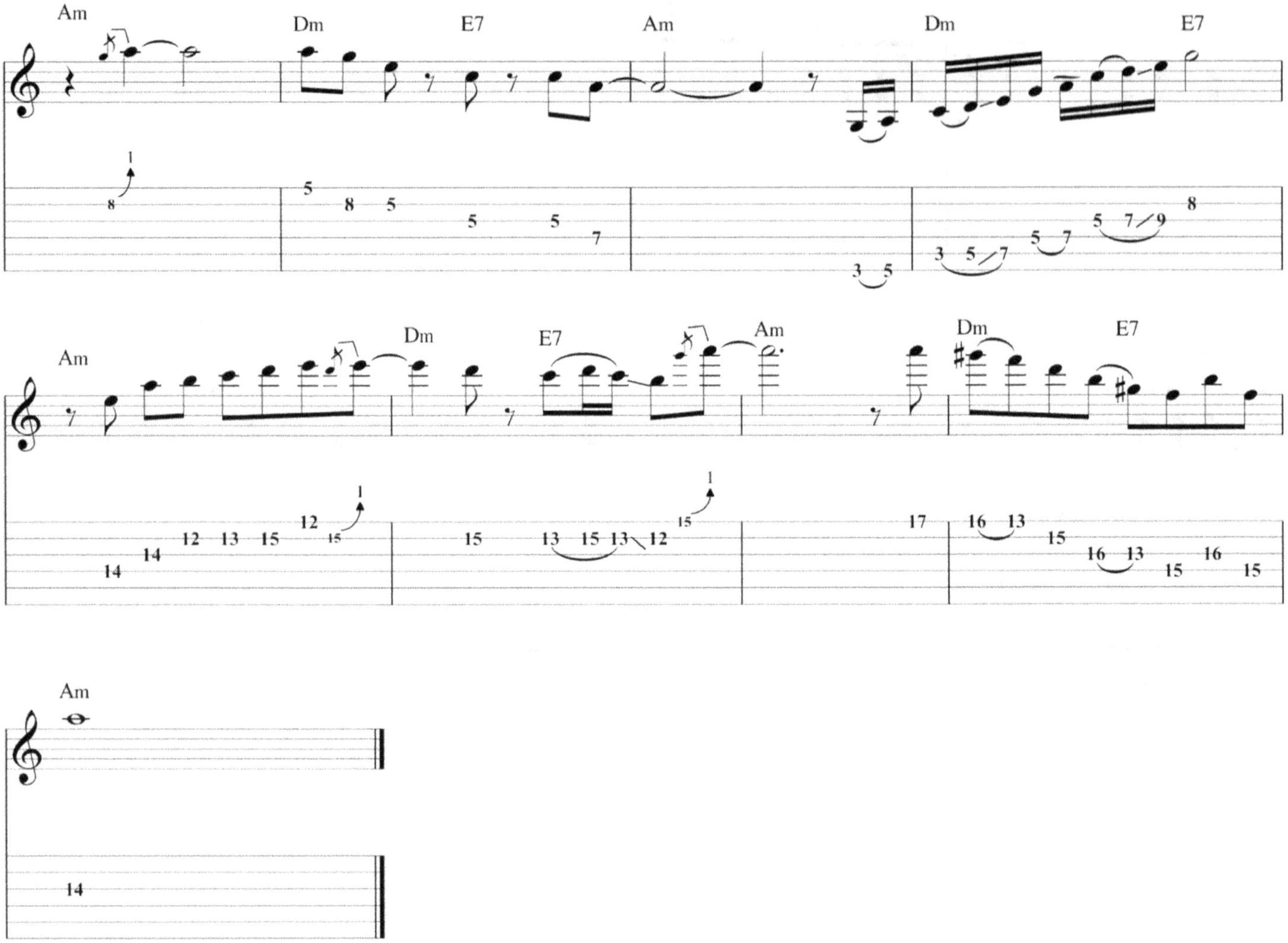
Am
Dm
E7
Am
Dm
E7
Am
Dm
E7
Am
Dm
E7
Am

# Chapter 3: Foo Fighters

**By Jamie Humphries**

The Foo Fighters are one of the most successful bands to emerge from Seattle's post-grunge scene. While drumming for Nirvana, Dave Grohl was quietly writing material, and after Kurt Cobain's death, he entered the studio to record the group's self-titled debut album. He'd played all the instruments on the record, so once the buzz began to spread, Grohl had to put a band together for live shows. Lineups have shifted over the years, but currently the band includes drummer Taylor Hawkins, bassist Nate Mendel, and guitarists Pat Smear and Chris Shiflett.

Mixing melodic hard rock with punk and blues elements, the Foos draw their influences from many bands and artists, including Black Flag, Queen, and Tom Petty. Their album *Sonic Highways* is an epic project that spawned a series of documentaries about legendary studios around the United States. The band spent a week in each studio's respective city, soaking up the area's culture and vibe before writing and recording a song inspired by the experience.

For this chapter, I've drawn ideas from such tracks as "My Hero," "Monkey Wrench," and "All My Life." We'll focus on tight power-chord riffs, chords that contain fretted notes and open strings, and melodic octave-based lines and figures.

The etude kicks off with a riff based on a standard B5 chord, but also throws in the open 5th string. Notice how the rhythm produces a very tight, punchy sound when locked in with the drums and bass. On the last beat of measures two and four, we give the harmony a bit of movement by throwing in a D5 and an E5. Simply shifting the start of a riff from beat 1 to beat 2 can really change a rhythm part's sound and feel. Check it out.

Our riff repeats in the next section, but we change the ending by going to an E/G# chord before hitting a huge E5 shape and then building tension with the D5 chord. The second half of the verse is mostly the same as the first eight measures, but with a simple twist: In the last measure, we move to a D6(sus2) to set up the chorus. This is a great demonstration of how you can embellish a basic power chord by simply including some open strings for added color. You should also notice that the second half of the verse concludes with an eighth-note rhythm as opposed to the tight 16th-note rhythm from measure eight.

Open strings play an essential part in the chorus riff that starts in measure 17. Throughout this section we let the top two strings ring out while moving chord shapes underneath. Check out how the A(sus2) chord comes in on beat 4 rather than the start of the next measure. The second half of the chorus goes from F#7(add11) to E5 (keep those open strings ringing) before returning to the D6(sus2).

The bridge starts with a melodic section that's reminiscent of the intro to "My Hero." For this, I composed a simple melodic figure based in E major (E–F#–G#–A–B–C#–D#) that continues to use the open 1st and 2nd strings to create some dissonance. As always: Where there's tension, there must be resolution.

Distorted octaves pop up in the last section. This progression is very similar to the verse, with the exception of the A(sus2) chord. The octave melody follows the rhythm of our accompanying riff, although in places it includes some fast 16th-note rhythmic ideas.

**Recording details.** Grohl's main guitar is his signature Gibson DG-335, but he also uses Explorers, Les Pauls, and even Telecasters on occasion. For our lesson, I played my Music Man Axis Super Sport guitar and a Music Man StingRay bass. I used Steinberg's Cubasis on my iPad to record the tracks, and Positive Grid's JamUp

Pro app provided the guitar and bass tones. For the guitar, I dialed up a model based on a Mesa/Boogie Dual Rectifier and a vintage Ampeg-style setting for the bass.

The drums were programmed with the Drums HD app, but I chopped a lot of the fills to create the final drum part. When it comes to Grohl's tone, opt for a thick overdrive sound, but avoid saturation—we need to hear those open strings!

**Example 3**

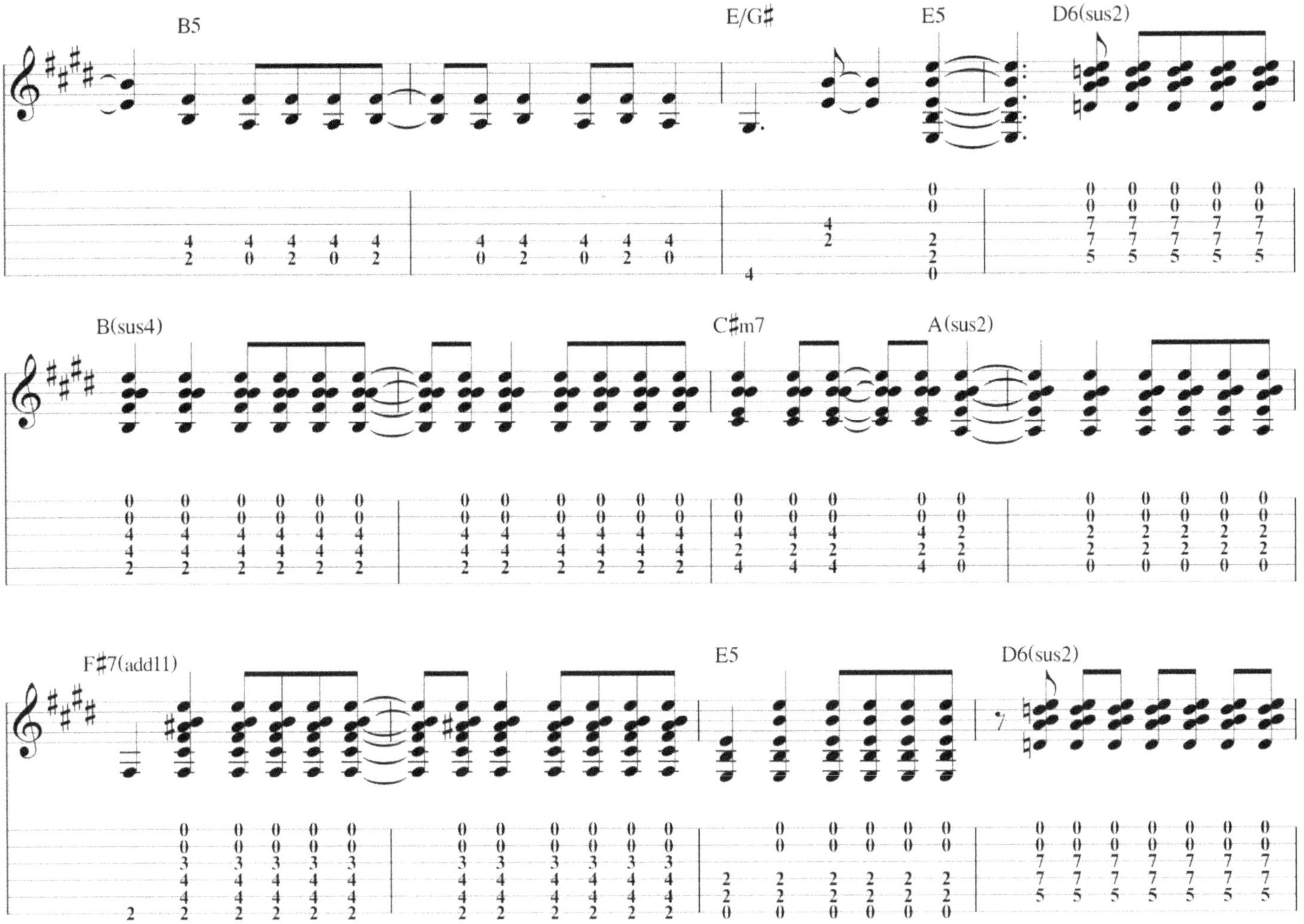
B5
E/G♯
E5
D6(sus2)
B(sus4)
C♯m7
A(sus2)
F♯7(add11)
E5
D6(sus2)

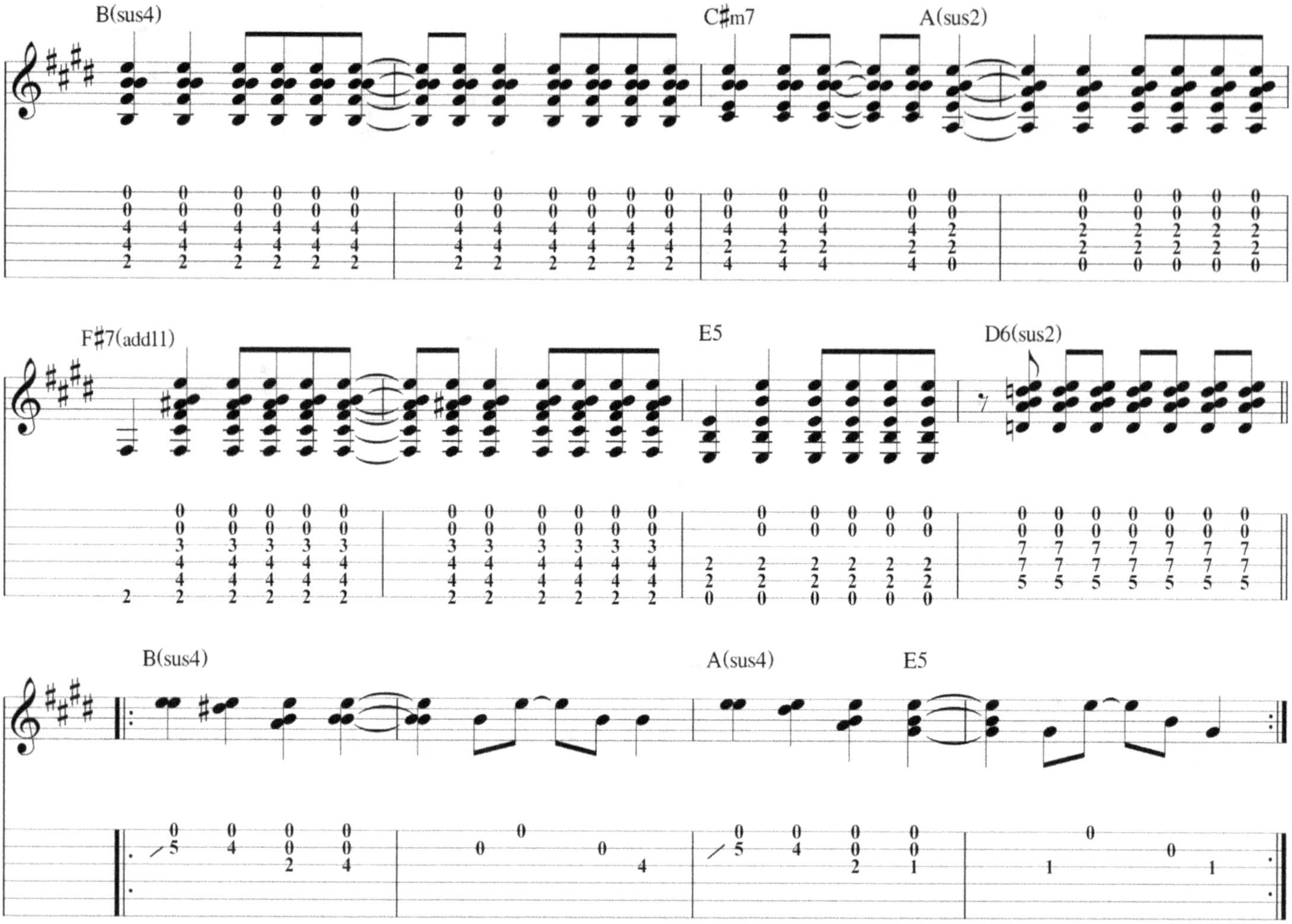
B(sus4)
C♯m7
A(sus2)
F♯7(add11)
E5
D6(sus2)
B(sus4)
A(sus4)
E5

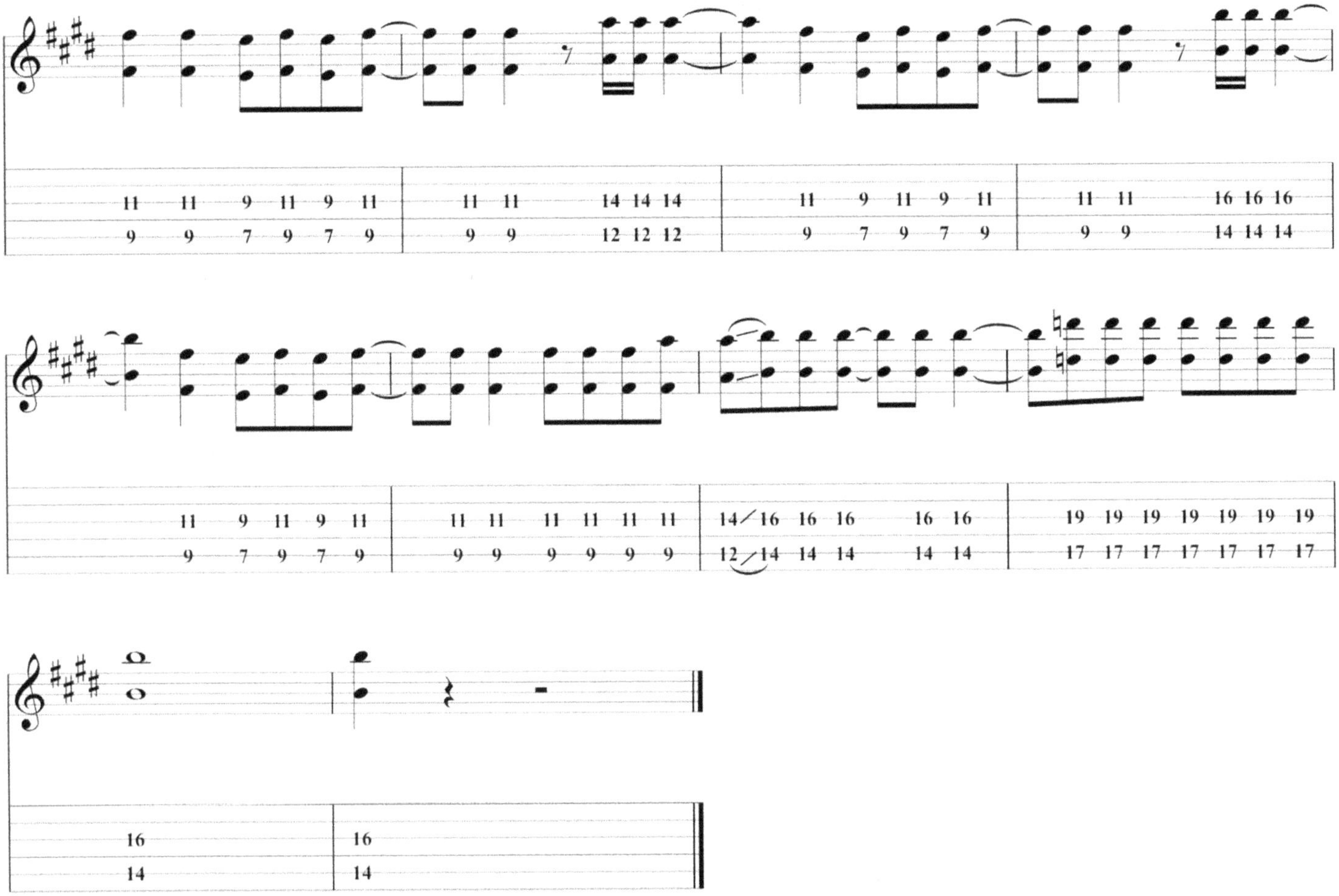

# Chapter 4: Brian May

## By Jamie Humphries

Now let's look at the unique guitar style of Dr. Brian May, from the legendary rock band Queen. May has been crafting distinctive guitar parts for more than 40 years, and Queen's popularity continues to grow with legions of loyal fans young and old. The band has inspired countless artists from Foo Fighters to Lady Gaga, and Queen's catalog includes some of the most popular classic rock tracks of all time.

Following the tragic and untimely death of the irreplaceable and enigmatic Freddie Mercury, the Queen legacy continues with May and drummer Roger Taylor flying the Queen flag at sold-out performances all over the world with singer Adam Lambert. They even have a live musical stage show *We Will Rock You*, which has enjoyed a nonstop run in London's West End for many years.

May has a unique style and favors some unorthodox techniques, such as attacking the strings with an old sixpence coin instead of a standard flatpick. He also uses his right-hand fingers a lot, either gently brushing across the strings or pulling his index finger off the strings as they rub against it. At first glance, you might think he's tapping.

In this lesson, I've tried to incorporate as many different rhythm and lead techniques as possible, and when composing this short piece I turned to a number of classic Queen songs for inspiration.

The first 10 measures are inspired by "Now I'm Here," from *Sheer Heart Attack*. This section features a slightly cleaner sound with the guitar volume backed off and some chorus to produce a wide-sounding effect. I work through a series of major triads while palm-muting the open 4th string. You can hear how the drums accent the chord stabs. I turn the volume up slightly for the conclusion of this section and work around an A5, D/A, and A7sus4 figure.

In the next section, we keep our verse riff and add some chordal ideas similar to what May played in "One Vision," off *A Kind of Magic*. These chords employ a very common characteristic of Brian's rhythm style, where the root note of a power chord simply drops down by a half-step to change the chord. I also put in a bit of the D blues scale (D–F–G–Ab–A–C) as well. Pay attention to the chord stabs and be sure to keep them tight and clean.

The driving figure that comes up next should sound familiar to anyone who has heard "Keep Yourself Alive" from Queen's debut album. I kick on a phaser for this section and conclude with some bluesy licks in G minor pentatonic (G–Bb–C–D–F). The next bit borrows elements from "Bohemian Rhapsody" and "Bicycle" with a quarter-note triplet before heading into a harmonized trill. The harmony idea continues with a descending line based around D major (D–E–F#–G–A–B–C#), leading us to the solo section.

The solo section moves to a half-time feel and the chord progression emulates Queen's majestic approach to ballads. May has an uncanny feel for melody and well-placed chord tones. The solo is based around F major and its diatonic modes, and the F major pentatonic (F–G–A–C–D) scale. Over the C/E chord, we touch on F#, which isn't diatonic to the key, but adds to the majestic sound. This section also features a fair amount of positions shifts, so take care with accuracy.

Next we explore some of May's signature scalar runs, starting off with triplets and then moving to 16th-notes. To give the backing track the correct feel, I've included some guitar harmony ideas, trying to emulate the sound of May's orchestrated lines. On the track there is some overlapping of lines. For example, in the second measure of this section, you'll notice that the guitar parts overlap a bit. I'll leave it up to you to choose which note to play.

The phrase over the Bb–Gm change includes a short melodic figure that sounds great attacked with the index finger for a smooth sound. The next bit is a common bluesy phrase that's based in C major pentatonic (C–D–E–G–A) with some passing tones. This lick works well over the C major to Bb/C chords and creates a dominant tonality. The final section includes an idea that May is famous for, and can be heard in the classic "Brighton Rock." Check out the ascending C Mixolydian (C–D–E–F–G–A–Bb) lines that use two different delay settings to produce a harmony. I set one delay to a half-note and another to a quarter-note, and both are synced to the track's tempo. As you climb up the scale, a harmony is produced as each delay enters.

May's main influences in his formative years included Hank Marvin and Rory Gallagher. Both guitarists had a profound effect on May's approach to tone. He has always favored Vox AC30 amps and started off with a Marvin-inspired clean tone. But he loved how Gallagher pushed his amp into a smooth overdrive using a treble booster to generate searing sustain. May has used this approach for many years, favoring the sound of the treble booster as it pushes the tubes harder. This produces saturation and sustain, but also cleans up the bottom end. May leaves his treble booster on all the time and to produce clean tones, he backs off his guitar's volume and plays lighter.

Live, May uses three modified Vox AC30s: The middle amp is completely dry and the left and right amps are dedicated to effects. The treble booster is in a small housing attached to his guitar strap and is routed before his wireless unit.

All these elements—plus the unique switching and tonal capabilities of May's "Red Special" guitar—go towards producing his signature tone. He also uses 6- and 12-string versions produced by Guyton guitars in the U.K., which are stunning instruments. I had the pleasure of using Brian's own green Guyton when I toured with him. Burns made some affordable replicas, but later Brian took over production with his own brand, Brian May Guitars.

**Recording details.** For the track, I used my own green Brian May production guitar, which has had a few modifications to it. This ran into a Brian May signature Fryer Treble Booster and then into a Wampler Thirty Something to emulate the front ends of the Vox. My amp is a Cornford Carrera, an 8-watt combo. The phaser is an MXR EVH 90, while the chorus, flanger, and delay were added in mixdown, courtesy of Line 6 Mod Pro and Echo Pro units. I used the guitar's volume to produce different amounts of gain or to make the tone clean, and the treble booster was on all the time. This track will obviously work with any guitar, but having the unique switching available on the Brian May guitar really helps emulate his sound: In some sections, I'd knock one pickup out of phase to produce that squawky tone and also help sonically separate the layered harmony lines.

# Example 4

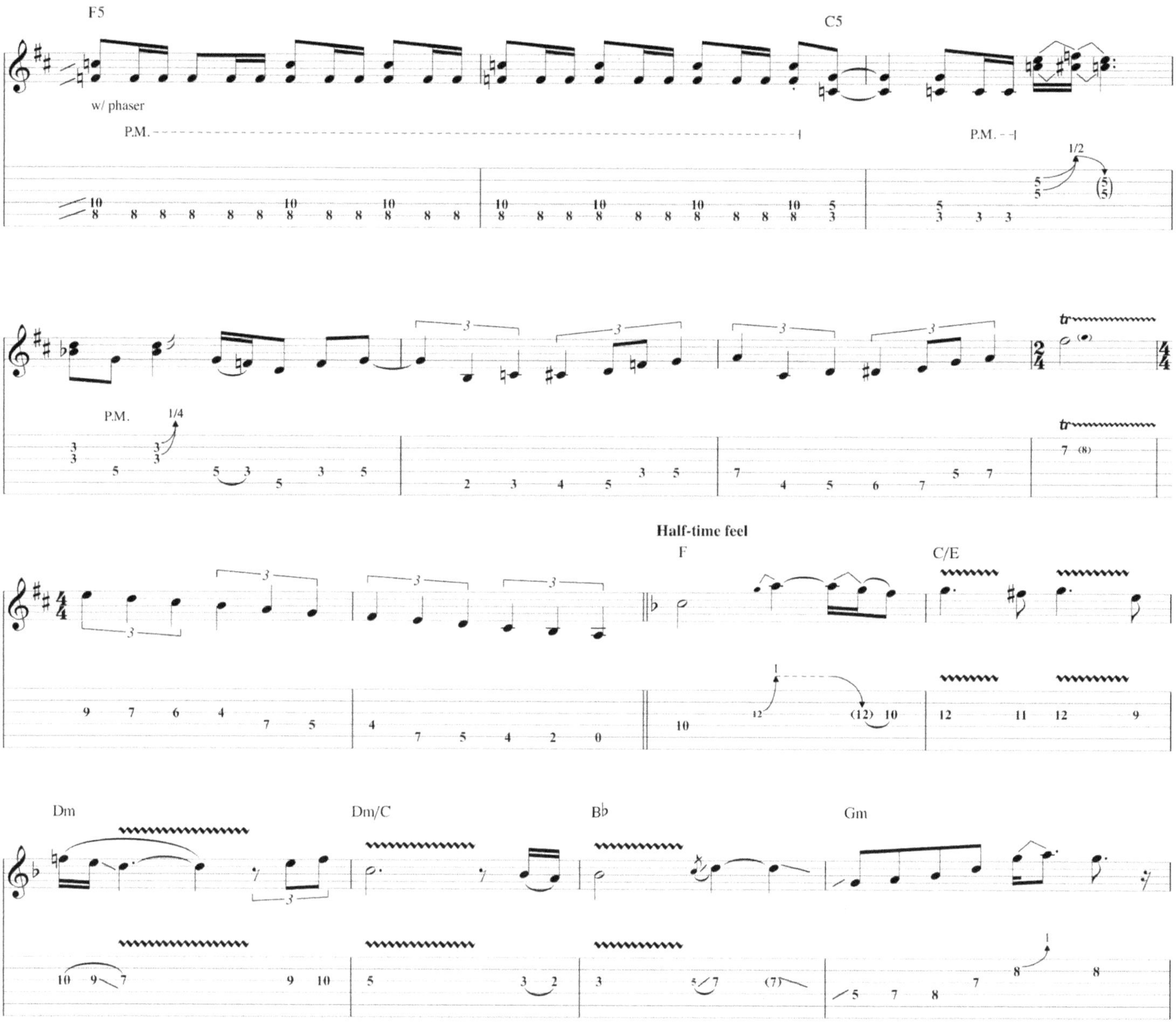
F5
C5
w/ phaser
P.M.
P.M.
1/2
P.M.
1/4
Half-time feel
F
C/E
Dm
Dm/C
B♭
Gm

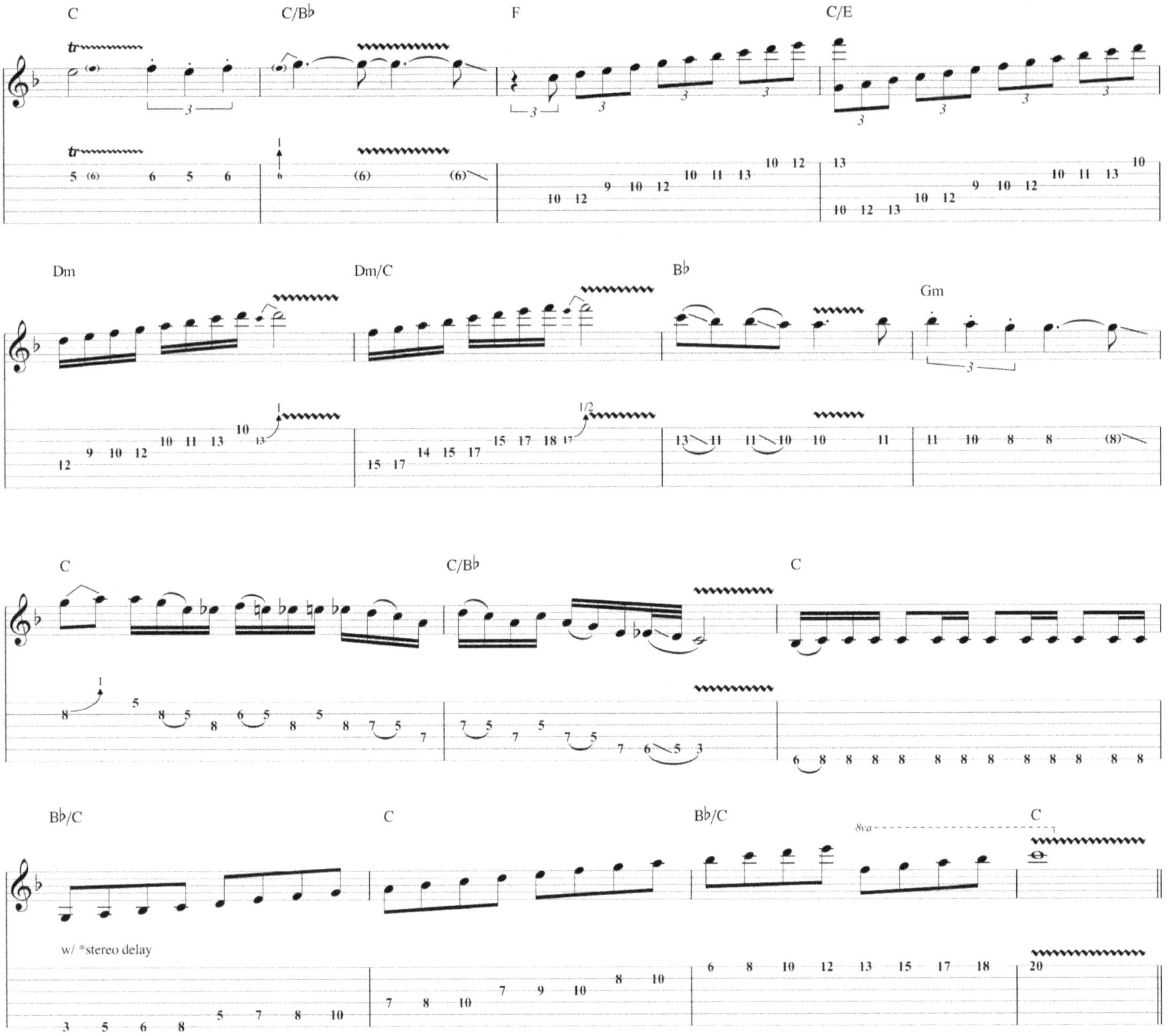


*Set for half note regeneration w/ one repeat.

# Chapter 5: U2's The Edge

## By Jamie Humphries

When it comes to unique and innovative voices on the guitar, The Edge is surely near the top of the list. His guitar parts are perfectly crafted, full of hooks, and offer an incredible amount of melody. He's also a master of creatively using effects in order to best serve the song. Often he'll start off with a very basic idea, but then add lush delays, modulation, and envelope effects to craft U2's signature soundscapes. In the recent documentary, *It Might Get Loud*, Jimmy Page describes Edge as a "sonic architect," which perfectly sums up Edge's approach to composition.

For this lesson, we'll focus on U2's classic era and borrow from such tunes as "Where the Streets Have No Name," "Sunday Bloody Sunday," "I Still Haven't Found What I'm Looking For," and "Pride (In the Name of Love)." The delay plays a large role in the sound and performance of the lesson track. I set my delay to a dotted-eighth-note at a tempo of 120 bpm.

Using this delay setting, the result sounds like a string of 16th-notes, even though you're only playing eighth-notes. But for the effect to work, it's vital that you stay totally in time. When setting up the delay, get a good balance between the dry and wet signals so that both are at the same volume level. To prevent the sound from getting cluttered and messy, use little or no feedback.

Most modern delay units let you set the tempo and note value, but if your device doesn't, simply use your ear. Play a staccato eighth-note rhythm and adjust the delay time until you get the desired 16th-note repeat. To ensure you're perfectly in time, use either the track or a metronome as your guide.

The Edge isn't the only guitarist to use this trick. Listen to David Gilmour, Albert Lee, Eddie Van Halen, and Nuno Bettencourt for more delay inspiration.

The intro starts off with a tight eighth-note rhythm similar to "I Still Haven't Found." Try using some palm muting to cut off the sustaining notes. Remember to pay attention to your timing or the 16th-notes won't come through.

In measure five, the verse progression kicks in. The chord-based melodic line sketches D–Bm–G, although the rhythm guitar is playing power chords. The figures that follow the power chords have a jangly vibe with a repetitive theme that adds to the hook—something that The Edge is known for. Make sure your picking hand is accurate and you don't strike unwanted strings.

The final two measures of the verse moves from a jangly strumming feel to a tight eighth-note figure against the delay. This figure is based around an A major chord, but implies A5 and Asus4. Pay attention to keeping perfect time during this section and play it with some light palm muting.

The chorus features an Em–G–D progression with a jangly strumming pattern that follows the underlying backing chords, but with more texture and color. Notice the syncopation created by rhythmic mutes that have been added to generate a tighter feel compared to the verse. Over the D chord, leave the 1st string open to ring throughout. This contrasts nicely with the previous two measures.

The Em returns before resolving to a held G5 chord. Before returning to the chorus again, play a series of harmonics at the 7th fret to build up tension. Thanks to the chiming harmonics and delay, this has a really cool U2 sound.

The next section, which has a subtle "Sunday Bloody Sunday" feel to it, outlines an Em–D–A progression. Once again, we encounter a chord figure that uses a series of two-note chords—or dyads—that follow the underlying power chords. Finally, end with a 16th-note pattern in the upper register over a D major chord.

The Edge uses a variety of different guitars, including Fender Strats and Teles, Gibson Les Pauls, Explorers, Rickenbackers, and occasionally Line 6 guitars. His main amp is usually a vintage Vox AC30, but his immense live rig also includes Marshall and Fender. As far as effects, he uses entirely too many to accurately list here, and he controls them all with a custom switching system.

**Recording details.** I cut this track using Steinberg's Cubasis for iPad with an Alesis iO Dock audio interface. Positive Grid's JamUp Pro supplied the guitar and bass tones, while the drums came from Drum Loops HD. I used a 5-string Music Man StingRay bass, and a Music Man Axis Super Sport for all the guitar parts. In JamUp, I dialed up a model of a Vox AC30 with some delay after the amp. In front of the amp, I added a MXR Dyna Comp-style compressor. For the crunch tones, I used a Hiwatt-style amp with a MXR Micro Amp model for extra drive.

**Example 5**

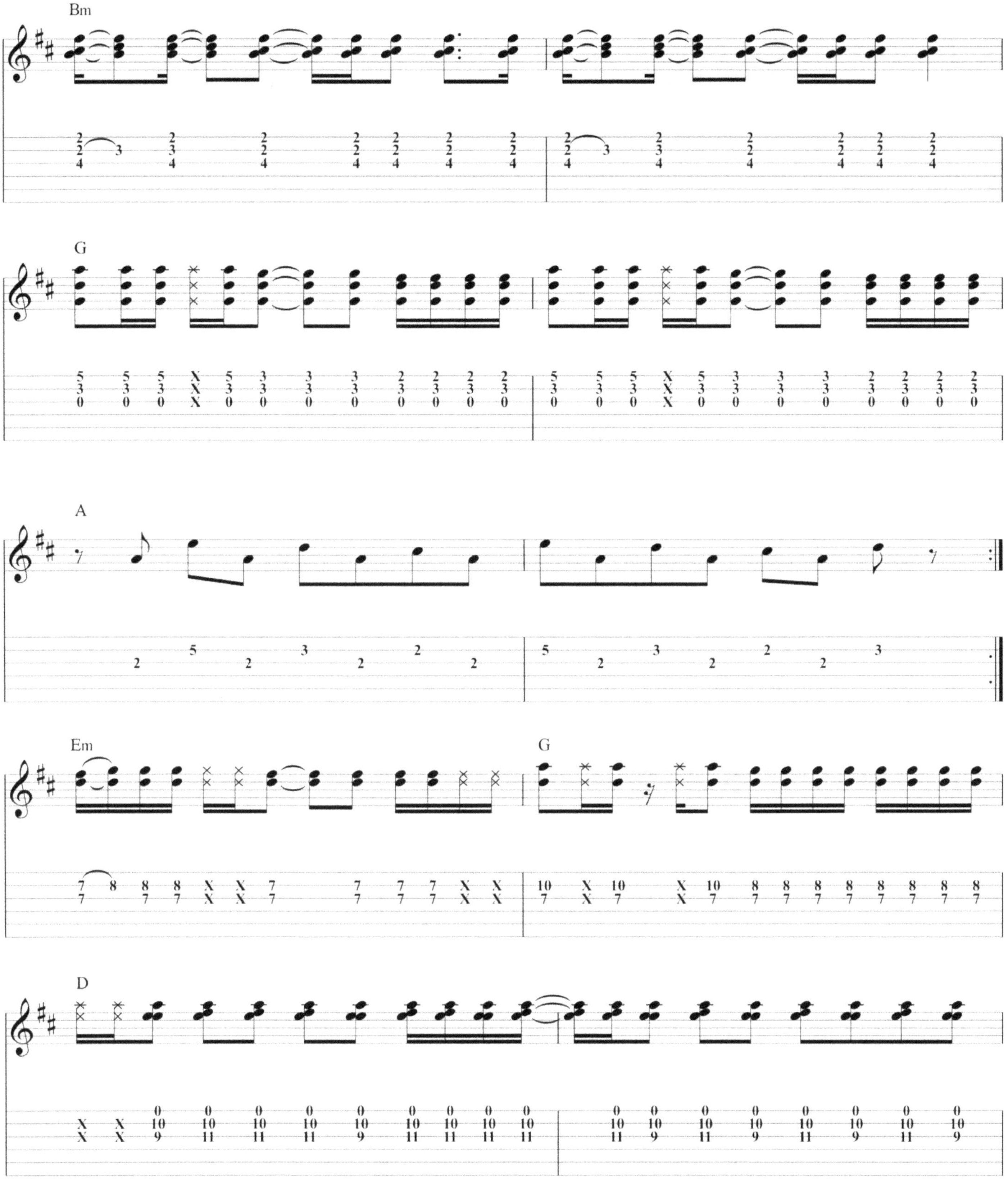
Bm
G
A
Em
G
D

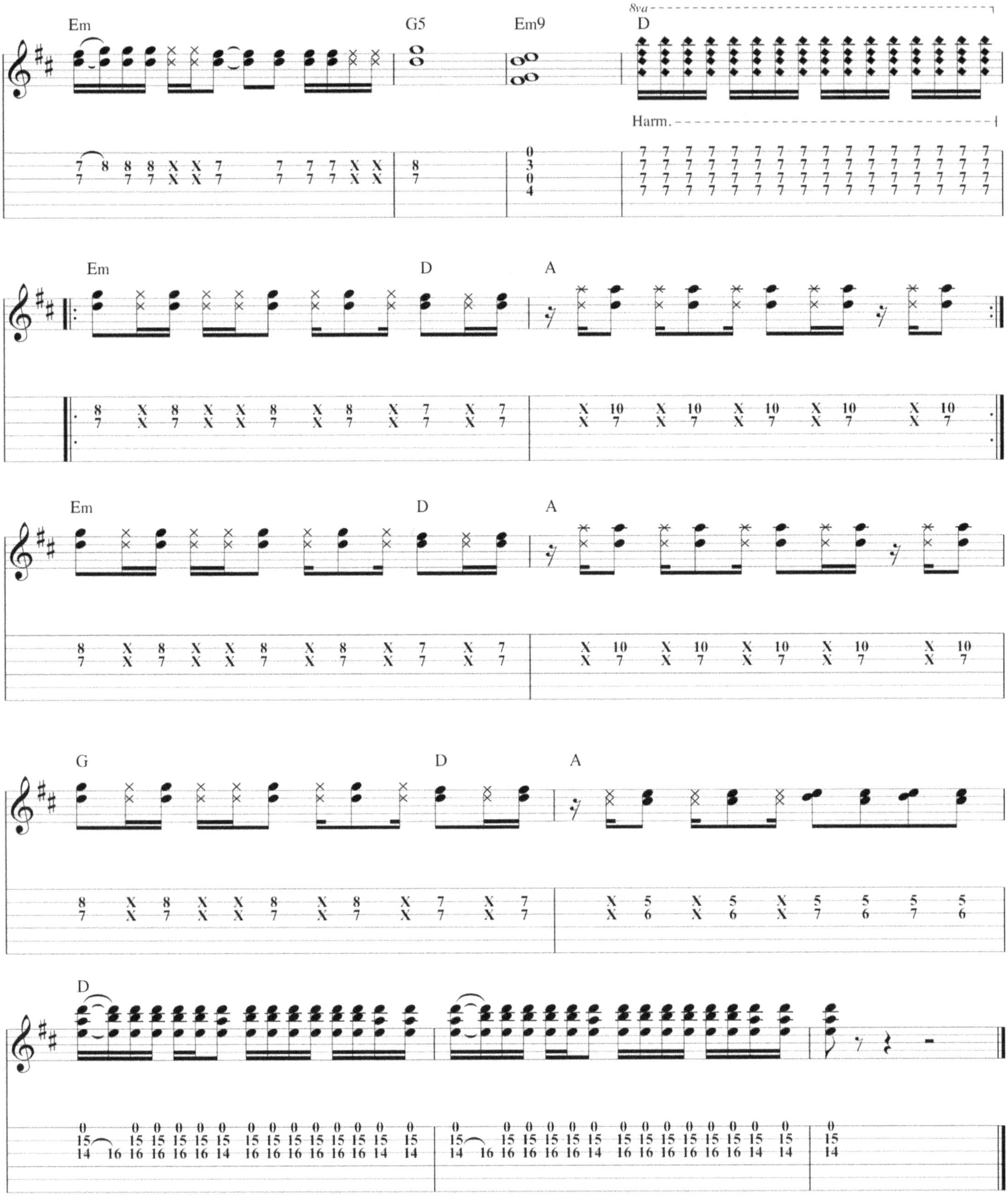
Em
G5
Em9
8va
D
Harm.
Em
D
A
Em
D
A
G
D
A
D

# Chapter 6: Jimmy Page

**By Jamie Humphries**

For this chapter, let's look at one of rock's most revered and influential guitarists, Jimmy Page. Not only did Page form one of the biggest-selling bands of all time, but his blend of American blues-style soloing and rock 'n' roll has inspired generations of guitarists and bands alike, and many point to him as the father of modern blues-rock and hard rock.

Page is one of those rare guitarists with an instantly recognizable sound. He was one of the first guitarists to use extended pentatonic riffs, fusing complex unison lines with the bass. He also showed his folk influences by experimenting with acoustic instruments and the very Eastern-sounding DADGAD tuning. He was a sonic pioneer too, employing a wide variety of effects and even playing his guitar with a violin bow.

Page recorded a wealth of material, so I want to cover as much stylistic variety as possible in this short study piece. The goal here is to demonstrate his riff style, use of triads, and also his approach to creating solos—namely position shifts and repetitive phrases.

The first eight measures of the verse are based around the power chords A5 and G5, with guitar and bass unison riffs that use notes from the A minor pentatonic scale (A–C–D–E–G). Notice the sprinkling of chromatic notes and check out the bluesy move from the b3 (C) to the major 3 (C#). The verse concludes with D and A/C# arpeggios.

For the beginning of the next section, I've tried to present an idea reminiscent of "Kashmir" without departing from regular tuning. As you play through this, you'll see that the open D on the 4th string remains constant below a series of descending triads before the phrase ends with a pair of Gm triads.

On the audio demo, I've opted for a slightly clean tone in this section, and I doubled the main guitar with a 12-string electric to create a jangly texture.

The solo section is inspired by "Stairway to Heaven" and uses the Am–Am/G–D/F# progression. (The Am/G is a chord many people play as a straight G chord.) The second half of the progression includes the chords Am, C, and D. The solo is based mainly around the A minor pentatonic scale, but also includes the b5 (Eb) to create the A blues scale, and adds the 6 (F#), which implies a Dorian sound. The solo kicks off with a classic blues-based bending figure that resolves to the F# note and outlines the D/F# chord. Measures 19-20 start with a classic Page repetition lick using bends and fast pull-offs. This lick is pretty hard to get smooth and clean, so build up speed gradually.

The phrase in measure 20 starts in A Dorian and shifts up a minor third—with the shape remaining the same—and turns into a cool blues-based lick. In the next few measures, you'll move through a few different pentatonic positions before hitting some high-register bends. The solo concludes with two classic Page-style moves: a repeating bending figure (this leads to the solo's climax) followed by a fast pull-off lick.

Page is known for using mainly a Gibson Les Paul or a Fender Telecaster, but also played a double-neck Gibson SG and a Danelectro. His amp selection was also varied. Everything from Marshalls, Supros, Oranges, and Hiwatts made appearances in the studio and onstage.

**Recording details.** I used several different guitars for this track, all of which ran into a Blackstar Series One 50 set to the clean-bright mode with the gain full and the Dynamic Power Reduction (DPR) set to about 10 watts. For the verse, I used my 1960 Fender Telecaster plugged into a Wampler Plexi-Drive for a little bite and grit. On the chorus, I ran the Tele straight into the Blackstar's clean-bright mode for some Class A-style breakup. I also doubled this with my 12-string electric, a Music Man BFR Silhouette. This sound was slightly cleaner and I added some phaser in the mix stage.

For the solo, I used my Music Man Axis Super Sport that's fitted with low-output DiMarzio 36th Anniversary PAFs. Still using the clean-bright mode, I plugged into the Plexi-Drive pedal and added a little extra gain, but rolled off some bottom end to make the tone slightly harsh.

Make sure you carefully study Page's tone because many people add too much gain. They hear what they *think* it is, but it's not. His tones were quite thin—fuzzy, in some places—but they worked perfectly in a mix.

**Example 6**

A5
D
A/C♯
G5
D(add4)
D
A/D
C/D
G/D
Gm/D
D(add4)
D
G/D
D(add4)
D
A/D
C/D
G/D
Gm/D
C
G/B
G
Am
Am/G
D/F♯
Am
C
D

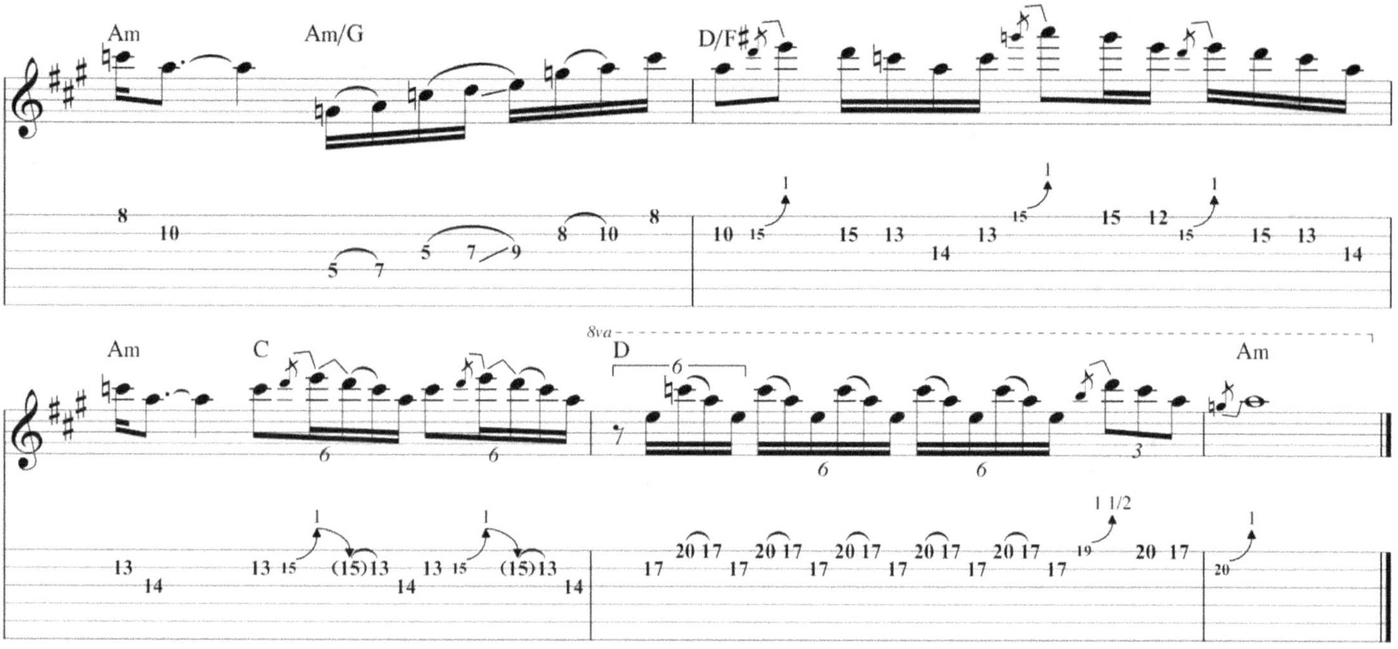
Am
Am/G
D/F♯
Am
C
8va
D
Am

# Chapter 7: David Gilmour

## By Jamie Humphries

Pink Floyd is without doubt one of the last remaining supergroups of the classic rock era. Like Queen, Led Zeppelin, and the Rolling Stones, Pink Floyd have sold millions of albums and filled arenas all around the world. The band started out as a psychedelic rock band, playing the underground clubs of London during the '60s, but later became one of the leaders of the progressive rock movement, composing complex songs with conceptual themes. These were performed against a backdrop of elaborate lighting, video projections, and inflatable stage props.

This piece was a joy for me, having been a fan of Floyd since I was a child. I also spent several years touring with the Australian Pink Floyd Show, and produced and mixed two albums for Roger Waters' current guitarist, David Kilminster. For this track, I drew inspiration from several famous Floyd songs, including "Breath," "Shine on You Crazy Diamond," and "Dog." The solo is a pastiche of many famous Gilmour licks.

The example kicks off with a verse that wanders through some C Lydian sounds (with the D/C chord) before resolving to C and modulating to G minor in the third measure. In Floyd's music, it isn't uncommon to subtly move through a few different key centers within a single section. The next section moves to the IIm chord in the key of F (Gm). The famous Gm6/Bb chord from the intro to "Shine on You Crazy Diamond" pops up in measure four. I simply couldn't resist playing this chord in a Floyd-style track. It makes for some cool harmonic coloring over the G minor tonality, and it's actually a lot easier than it sounds. (I've even seen it taught using all fretted notes and no open strings!)

In the next section of the verse, we pick up some rhythmic and harmonic moves from "Dogs." Here, I'm using a simple Fmaj7 chord shape in the 1st position, but the D played by the bass gives it a Dm9 sound. I then move that shape up a few frets and play an Abmaj7, but again, the F from the bass yields a Fm9 sound. This technique reapplying basic chords against a new root is a great way to get different sounds.

A "Breath"-inspired chorus is up next and begins with a strummed Em(add9) chord and some higher-positioned open chords over the A7. The next measure contains some simple C and D chords before repeating the Em–A7 section again.

A descending chord progression that's borrowed from "Shine On" leads into the solo. I particularly like the relationship between the Dm, Dm/C, and the Bm7b5, as you'll notice they all include the Dm triad played on the 4th, 3rd, and 2nd strings with just the root note shifting. Again, this is a great writing tool to explore.

An A minor blues progression forms the harmonic foundation for the solo. For a twist, the turnaround is F, E7#9, Dm7, C, and G/B. Most of the melodic elements are based around the A minor pentatonic (A–C–D–E–G) scale. The key to Gilmour's style is his laid-back feel—make sure not to rush!

Gilmour's signature pull-off figure from "Shine On" appears in the fourth measure of the solo. This section also includes some tricky bends, including some pre-bends. One of Gilmour's favorite bends happens in the fifth measure with a two-step stretch. The solo then moves down into the very familiar 5th position for some licks based off the A blues scale (A–C–D–Eb–E–G). The solo concludes with a nod to "Comfortably Numb" when the 9 (B) gets added to the pentatonic scale.

David Gilmour is known for having one of the best tones in rock. He uses various Hiwatt amps with an elaborate effects system that includes a variety of stompboxes and rack equipment. (At one time he even used modified Alembic bass amps that were combined with a crossover system that allowed the Hiwatts to handle the upper frequencies while the Alembics covered lower frequencies.) Gilmour mainly plays his famous black Fender Strat, although he's used a Tele and a P-90-equipped Les Paul. I'd suggest checking out gilmourish. com, which I found to be an invaluable resource when building my rig for the Aussie Floyd tours.

**Recording details.** I used Steinberg's Cubasis for iPad to record this track. For the drums, I either program them in Cubasis (which has really great samples) or, as in the case here, I use an app called Drum Loops HD, which offers a variety of styles recorded with modern and vintage mics. The bass is tracked live with a Music Man StingRay 5 plugged into Positive Grid's JamUp Pro app via an Apogee interface. For the bass amp, I used a model based on an old '60s Ampeg. On the guitar side, I grabbed my trusty Ernie Ball Music Man Axis Super Sport. I used a single-coil configuration for the clean tones and the neck humbucker for the solo. I rolled off the volume a bit to emulate a P-90-style tone. Again, I used JamUp Pro for the guitar sounds and dialed up a Hiwatt-style amp with some spring reverb and an Echoplex-style effect.

For the "Shine On" chords, I used a different single-coil setting on the guitar through emulated MXR Dyna Comp and Uni-Vibe effects. For the solo, I added a touch of front-end bite with a fuzz pedal and a flanger modeled after a vintage Electro-Harmonix pedal. I also increased the amount of delay and reverb during the solo for a more ethereal tone. The "acoustic guitar" in the background was the piezo pickup on the Axis through an acoustic DI and acoustic amp in JamUp.

## Example 7

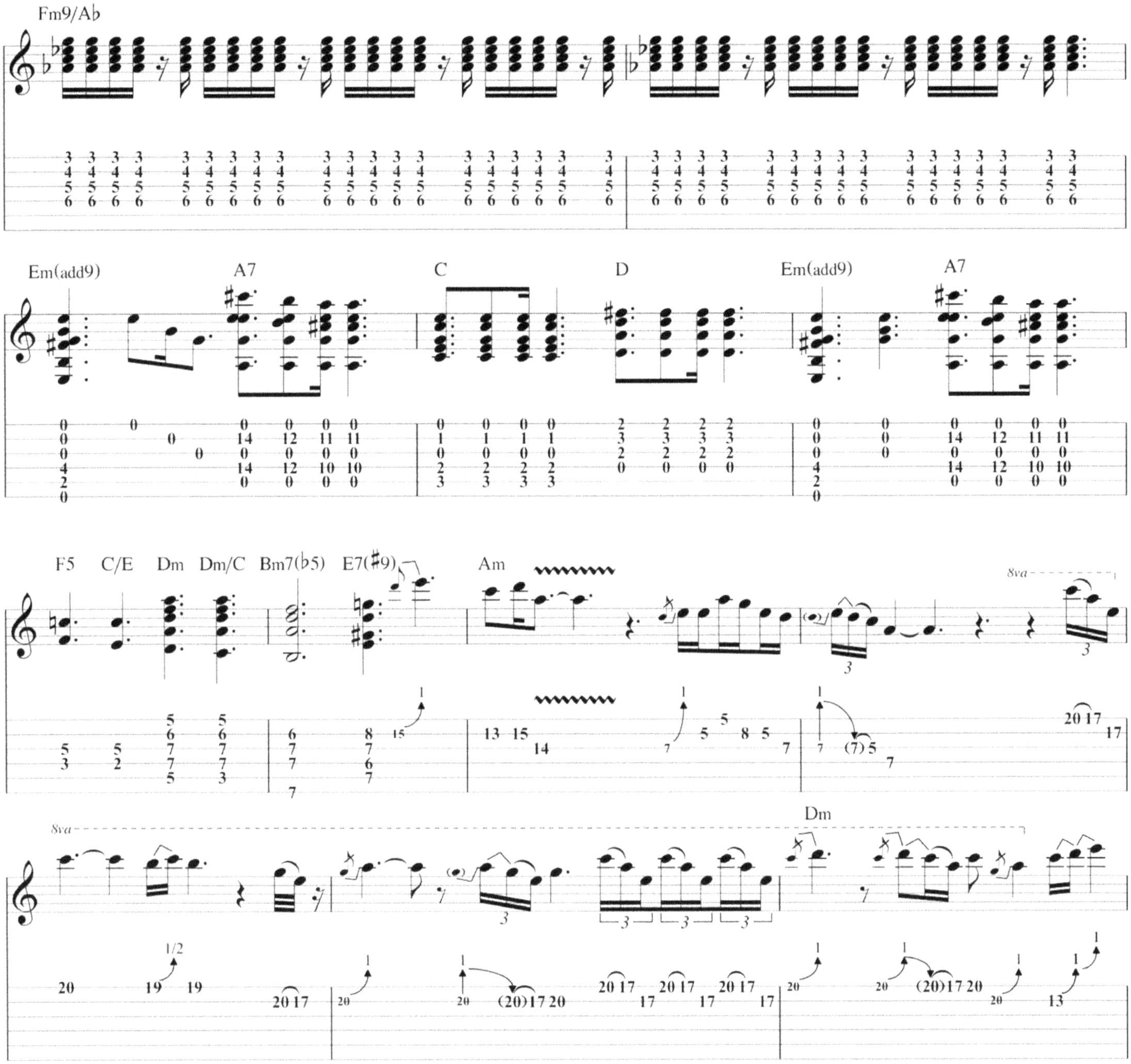
Fm9/A♭
Em(add9)
A7
C
D
Em(add9)
A7
F5
C/E
Dm
Dm/C
Bm7(♭5)
E7(♯9)
Am
8va
8va
Dm

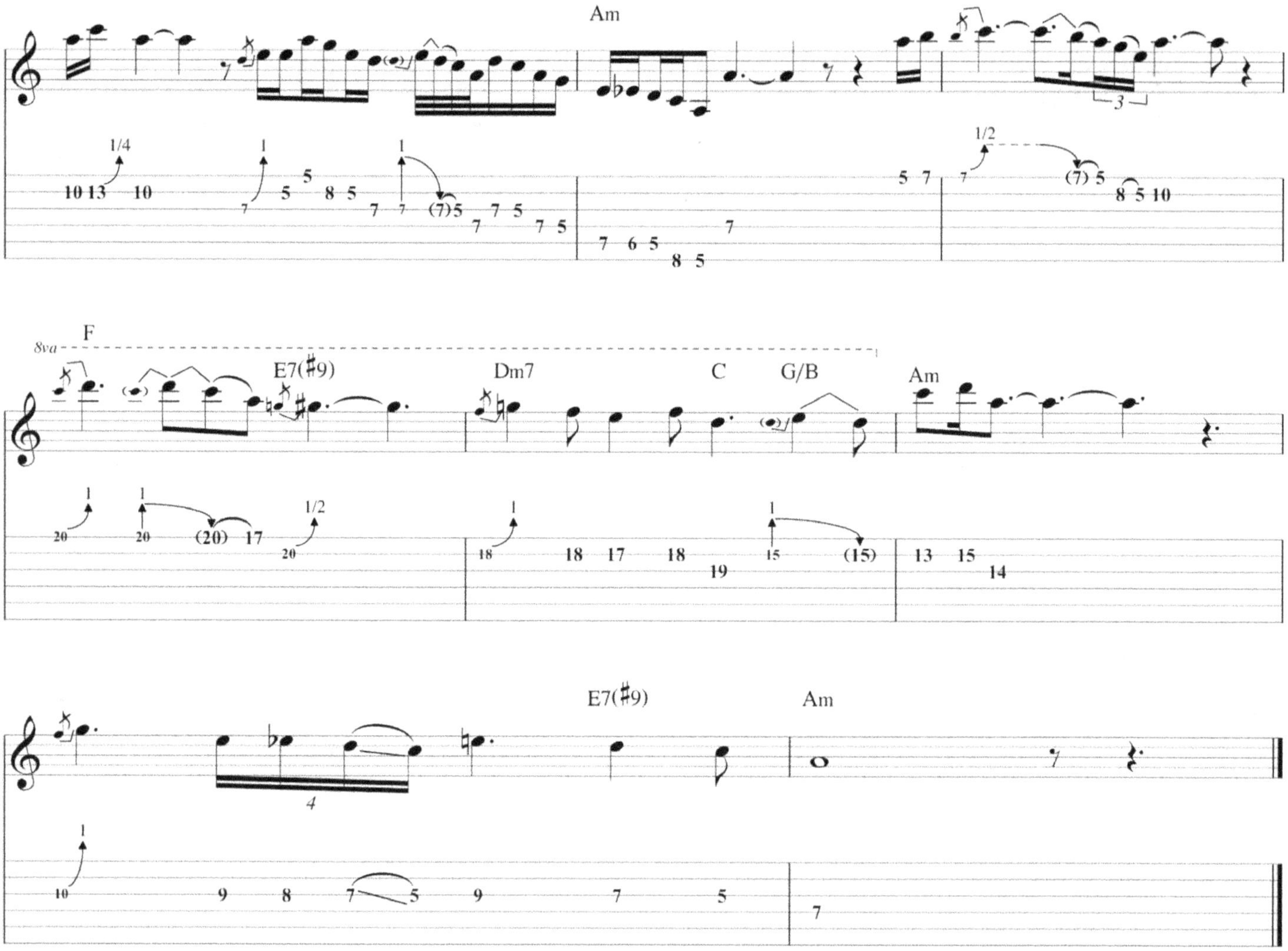
Am
8va
F
E7(♯9)
Dm7
C
G/B
Am
E7(♯9)
Am

# Chapter 8: Steve Morse

**By Jamie Humphries**

In this chapter we're going to take a look at the music of Steve Morse, one of the most versatile rock guitarists in history. Morse is known for his exceptional rock technique, but he's equally at home playing country, bluegrass, jazz, or classical.

Morse first established his reputation via the Dixie Dregs, a rock-inspired jazz group he formed shortly after graduating from the University of Miami with bassist Andy West. The band released several critically acclaimed albums, and then disbanded following 1982's *Industry Standard*. During the '80s, Morse recorded a string of solo albums, and then joined the prog-rock band Kansas in 1986.

In 1994, Morse joined Deep Purple after original guitarist Ritchie Blackmore departed. (Joe Satriani replaced Blackmore for a portion of *The Battle Rages On* tour.) After recording five studio albums, seven live albums, and performing countless shows, Morse has now occupied Deep Purple's guitar chair longer than Blackmore.

A master technician, Steve Morse is lauded for his impressive picking chops, ability to create flowing lines, and playing arpeggios at blistering speed.

Morse also makes use of artificial harmonics, open chord voicings, synth-like tones, and pad-like swells. One of the best examples of his country influences is "The Bash," a two-beat country jam from the 1979 Dixie Dregs album, *Night of the Living Dregs*. His unique approach also crossed over to the construction of his instrument. In his search for an instrument to cover rock and country tones, Morse configured a Tele with two humbuckers and two single-coils. This instrument served as the inspiration for his current Ernie Ball signature model axe.

When composing our lesson track, I was inspired by "Take It off the Top," "User Friendly," and "StressFest." This piece features picking sequences, triad-based riffs, and a bluesy solo that incorporates chromatic lines and country-inspired bends.

The example kicks off with a 16th-note picking sequence over D5 and E5 chords. The sequence outlines D Lydian (D–E–F#–G#–A–B–C#) over the D5 chord and E Mixolydian (E–F#–G#–A–B–C#–D) over the E5 chord. I've also doubled the picking figure with a piano, as Morse often blends a synth sound with his guitar signal. Notice that every note is picked—a hallmark of Morse's style—but if you find the tempo too challenging, try including some pull-offs.

The verse riff is almost entirely based around a series of triads similar to what you might hear on Morse's "Take It off the Top." It starts with the V, IV, and I triads in the key of A (E, D, and A, respectively) before borrowing a pair of chords from the key of F (F/A and C/G). The verse concludes with a descending unison lick that flows through the E minor pentatonic scale (E–G–A–B–D). This section repeats again with a slight variation before going into an interlude ahead of the solo.

In the middle section, the rhythm guitar plays around with *quartal* harmony, or chords stacked in fourths instead of thirds. When you listen to the backing track you can hear how these shapes produce a very modern, ambiguous sound. The main guitar works up the neck with a series of angular arpeggios. In the final two measures before the solo, check out the triplet-based lick that outlines an A major triad (A–C#–E) and a B major triad (B–D#–F#).

The solo begins with some country bends that mix major and minor pentatonic sounds. Hold the 2nd string bend with your second and third fingers while reaching for the notes on the 1st string with your fourth and first fingers—very Nashville. Morse's speed-picking chops come into play with a fast alternate-picked line that leads into a simple blues lick based in the E minor pentatonic box. Check out the E note played on the 6th string—try to grab it with your fretting-hand thumb. The next two measures feature a signature, twisted blues lick that combines elements of the Dorian and blues scales. Finally, the solo ends with another palm-muted lick that offers plenty of chromaticism.

As I mentioned before, Morse isn't afraid to chart his own path when it comes to his gear. Usually, Morse uses his signature Ernie Ball guitar with a few of his signature Engl E656 amps. The amps are configured in a wet/dry setup, and Morse controls the delay in the wet amp with an Ernie Ball volume pedal.

**Recording details.** For this session I used my Music Man Axis Super Sport (fitted with DiMarzio 36th Anniversary PAF pickups) through a Marshall JMP1 tube preamp. I kicked on a Wampler Plexi-Drive for the solo. I also added some delay during mixing.

## Example 8

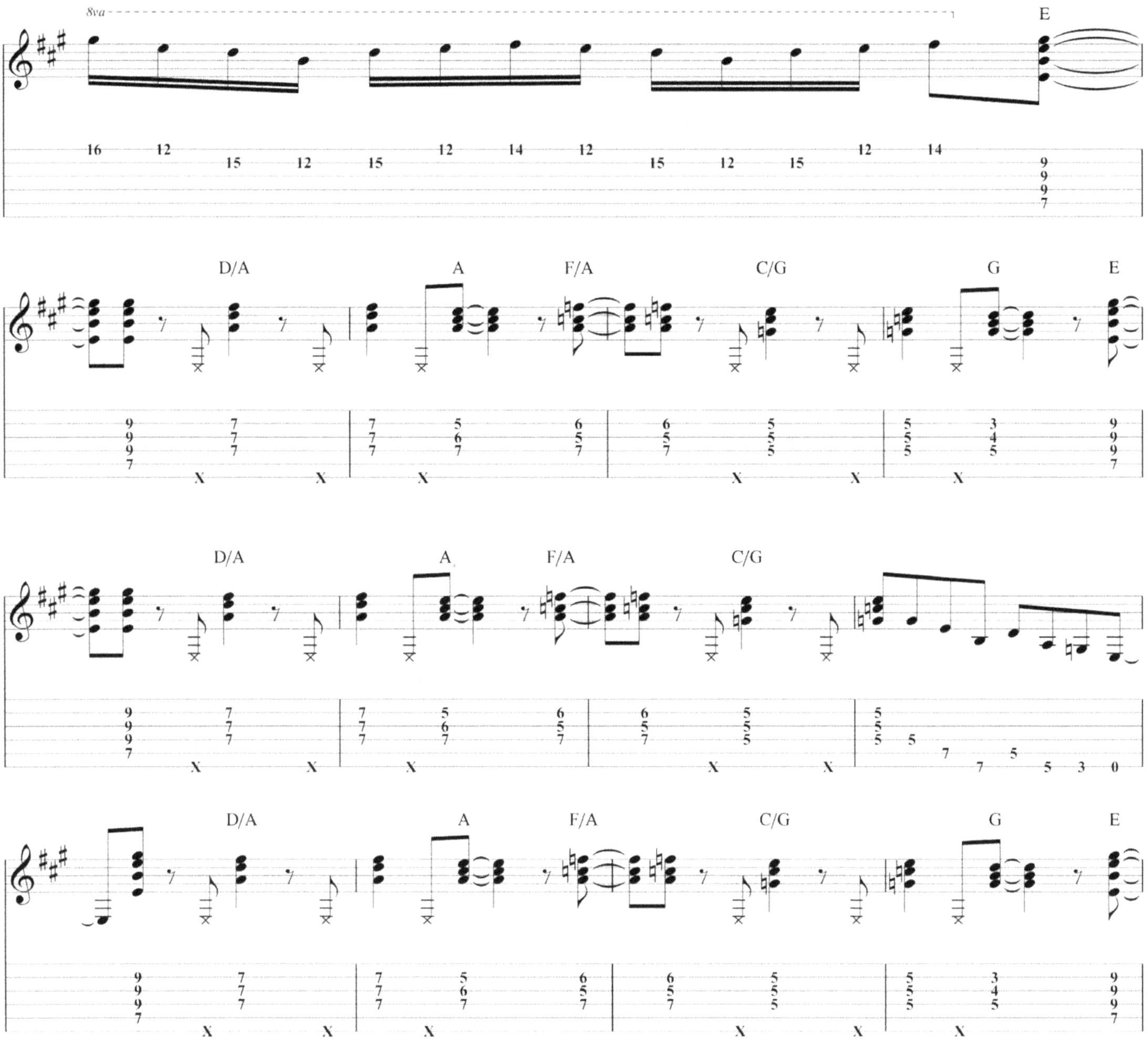
8va
E
D/A A F/A C/G G E
D/A A F/A C/G
D/A A F/A C/G G E

D/A A F/A C/G G
D/F♯ E/G♯ F/A G/B A/C♯ B/D♯ E
D/A A5 D/F♯
A D/A A E D/A A5
8va
P.M.
A5 D/F♯ A5 D/A A E5
P.M.

# Chapter 9: John McLaughlin

## By Shawn Persinger

What do you get when you cross odd meters with synthetic modes, displaced accents, Eastern philosophy, Marshall amps, and unbridled energy? Unfortunately, most of us would just get a mess of noise, but if you're John McLaughlin, you get the essence of the Mahavishnu Orchestra and some of the most revolutionary music to come out of the 20th century.

In *The 50 Greatest Guitar Books* I wrote extensively about how *The Inner Mounting Flame*, Mahavishnu Orchestra's debut recording, literally changed my life overnight, so I won't retell that story here. Nevertheless, it's worth saying that hearing John McLaughlin's music for the first time was a pivotal moment, and I am delighted to have been given this opportunity to try to relate some of his musical concepts to you.

McLaughlin's musical legacy is vast in scope and material. Thus, this lesson focuses on only one aspect of his 50-year career, specifically the original incarnation of the Mahavishnu Orchestra, which lasted from 1971 to 1973. Yet even limiting ourselves to just three years and three albums gives us an enormous number of musical concepts to explore, so let's get started.

To grasp McLaughlin's playing and compositional style, it's essential to have a basic understanding of modes. While space limits us from exploring modes in depth, the first few examples provide insight into the variations one can create from basic scales. For our examples, we'll stay in the 12th position and base our fingerings on an E tonality. In **Example 9a**, you can see a basic fingering for the E natural minor scale, otherwise known as E Aeolian (E–F#–G–A–B–C–D).

**Example 9a**

**Example 9b** illustrates the harmonic minor variation. There are several different ways to think of E harmonic minor (E–F#–G–A–B–C–D#), but for our purposes we will consider this an Aeolian scale with a natural 7 (D#).

**Example 9b**

Example 9c is what McLaughlin calls a "synthetic scale," or a scale that doesn't occur natively in Western scales and modes. He describes it as the "double harmonic minor" scale. Basically, it's a harmonic minor with an added b5 or "blue" note—in this case, Bb.

It's worth mentioning that in *John McLaughlin and the Mahavishnu Orchestra* scorebook, McLaughlin includes no fewer than 16 synthetic modes as points of reference "for the benefit of the serious music student."

**Example 9c**

Example 9d is where things start to get interesting. This is a classic McLaughlin-esque arpeggio figure that uses notes from all of the aforementioned scales, thus giving us nine different notes to work with. But it gets even better! Since the arpeggio starts and ends on B, we are actually playing in a synthetic version of B Phrygian dominant (B–C–D#–E–F#–G–A), which is a mode found in the E harmonic minor scale.

**Example 9d**

If all of this seems needlessly confusing—I hear you screaming—I would agree … up to a point. But it is important to remember that McLaughlin knows, understands, and uses all of these concepts in his playing and composing. So if you want your own music to be unique and innovative, a little knowledge (confusing as it may be at first) can go a long way.

The modes are just the start of what makes this unusual arpeggio pattern so unique. The next aspect to consider is the rhythm McLaughlin used. The time signature here is 5/4, a meter that appears throughout Paul Desmond's "Take Five" and in portions of the theme to *Mission Impossible* by Lalo Schifrin. McLaughlin has a habit of making his odd meters even more challenging by displacing the accents of his bass notes, which I have also done here. You'll hear these displaced accents throughout McLaughlin's career, most notably in the Mahavishnu pieces "The Dance of Maya" and "Hope."

Moving on to our melody (**Example 9e**), we revisit our modes and find a highly syncopated line played in octaves (one guitar is played up an octave to emulate the register of Mahavishnu violinist Jerry Goodman) using notes from the B Phrygian dominant scale. (Remember, that's also the E harmonic minor scale.) This melody or *head*, as jazz musicians call it, is slow enough to be recognized as a theme but too angular, syncopated, and dissonant to be called catchy. But who needs catchy when you can have angularity, syncopation, and dissonance?

**Example 9e**

Finally, we put everything together and add in the solo (**Example 9f**). Ironically, there's not much theory to discuss, though there are plenty of stylistic details to absorb. Personally, I'm of the opinion that when it comes time to solo over a Mahavishnu tune, McLaughlin lets go of his modal concepts and becomes a much more intuitive player. He frequently plays pentatonic lines over his modal arpeggios, letting the harmony do the work of establishing the exotic mode, while he solos more like a hyper-speed Hendrix than a technically precise music theoretician. When it comes to McLaughlin's Mahavishnu soloing, the term "reckless precision" has never been more apt.

The solo highlights several of McLaughlin's signature licks and concepts, including his use of *accelerando*, or speeding up (measures two, five, and six of the solo), repetitive licks, and playing on the lower strings in the higher register. And, of course, extreme speed and syncopation.

**Example 9f**

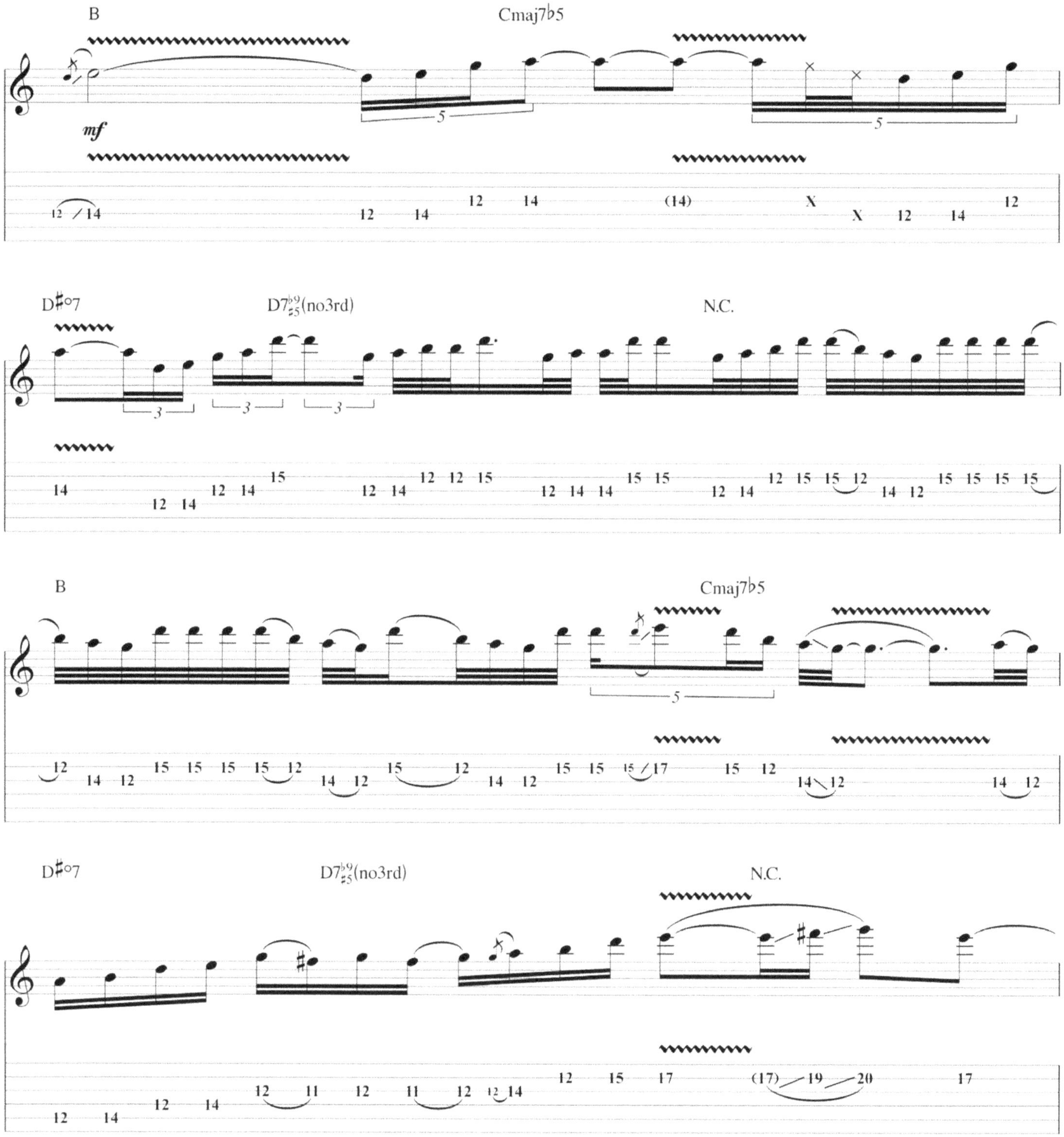
B
Cmaj7♭5
mf
D♯°7
D7♭9♯5(no3rd)
N.C.
B
Cmaj7♭5
D♯°7
D7♭9♯5(no3rd)
N.C.

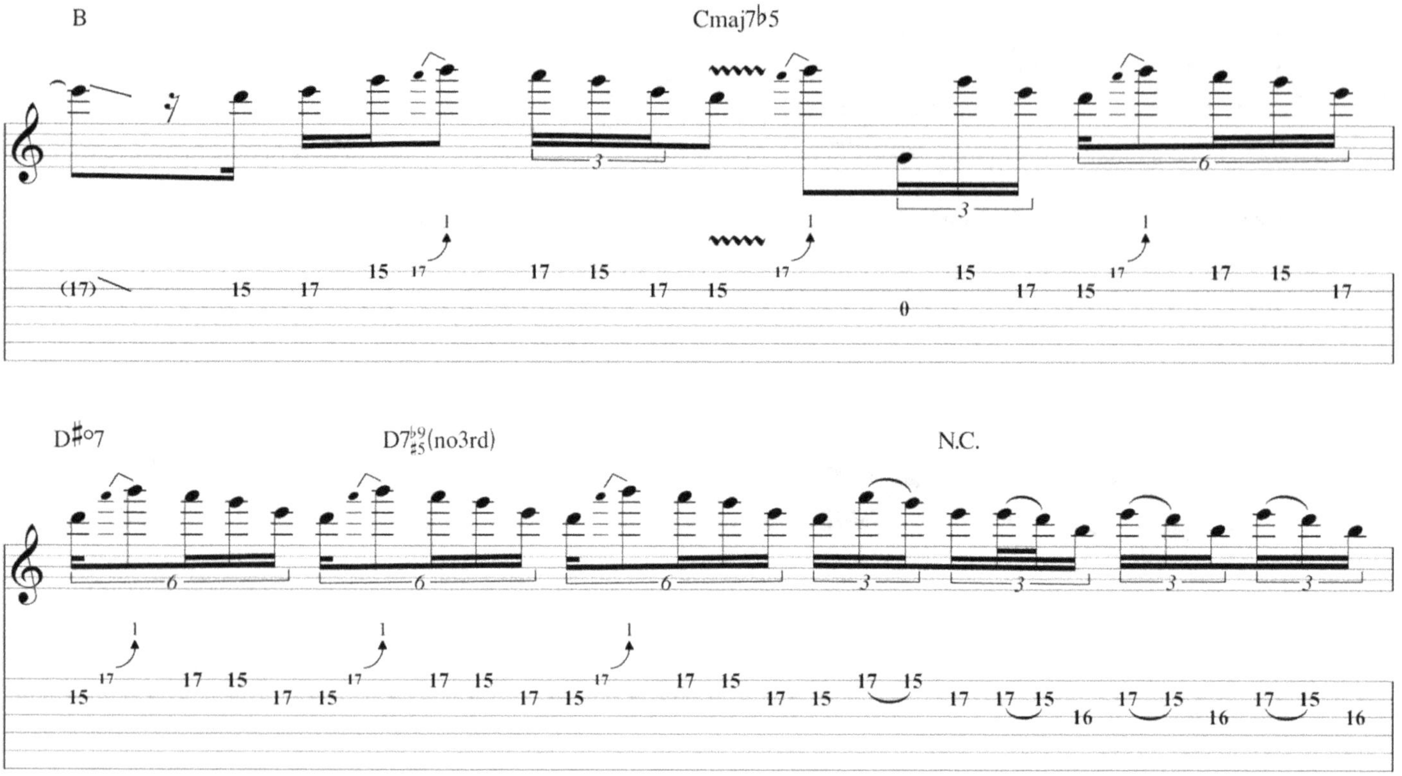
B
Cmaj7♭5
D♯o7
D7♭9♯5(no3rd)
N.C.

You can see that it's not any *one* concept that makes John McLaughlin's playing unique. Rather it's his liberal use of a multitude of influences, both musical and philosophical—rock and jazz, East and West, logic and intuition—that creates his inimitable style. If you hope to attain any resemblance to McLaughlin, you must open your mind, open your heart, and practice, practice, practice.

# Chapter 10: Jerry Garcia

## By Shawn Persinger

Possessing an immediately recognizable tone, a knack for inventing playful melodies, and a skillful technique (often overshadowed by his iconic personality), Jerry Garcia epitomizes personal expression on guitar. With more than 15,000 hours of playing documented, Garcia remains one of the most recorded guitarists in history. Thus, it can be difficult to know where to start when discussing his eclectic style, which embraced folk, blues, country, rock, jazz, and the avant-garde.

This etude will focus on Garcia's playing style from his time in the Grateful Dead—his most celebrated context. While this lesson highlights his single-note playing, you should keep in mind that all members of the Grateful Dead had a hand in creating the band's music. Garcia was constantly reacting—both with and against—the notes and rhythms played by the rest of the band. That said, I've chosen to keep the chord progression and rhythm of this lesson to a Grateful Dead staple: the simple two-chord Mixolydian jam.

First of all, what is a Mixolydian jam? This progression vamps from B to A. These chords are actually the V and IV in the key of E, so we'll consider that our "home base" even though we never hit an E chord. This demonstrates the relationship between the Ionian (1–2–3–4–5–6–7) and Mixolydian (1–2–3–4–5–6–b7) modes. Just compare E Ionian to B Mixolydian and you'll see the scales contain exactly the same notes; they simply start in a different spot. The V–IV progression certainly creates a happy major sound, but it's not sugary sweet, *pop* happy. It's more like, "Hey relax, chill out."

We'll solo using notes from the E major scale (E–F#–G#–A–B–C#–D#) enhanced with a few chromatic passing tones. The sound of this V–IV progression is very common in many Dead songs. Check out the funky, envelope filter-driven groove of "Fire on the Mountain" or the legendary improvisational juggernaut, "Dark Star."

Typically, Garcia solos tend to be quite lengthy, some as many as 10 minutes long. This allowed Garcia to develop his solos slowly and rather methodically. For our limited space here, I've condensed the idea of a thematically developed solo into four different sections, each eight measures in length.

The first measure introduces a classic Garcia concept—a simple motif consisting of diatonic thirds that then moves down a whole-step. Garcia would repeat and transform an idea like this, presenting several variations on the lick. This motif is turned and twisted in several other places in the etude.

The third and sixth measures contain what I think of as the definitive Garcia lick, the chromatic slur. You can see the lick moves chromatically down from B to G# and although it only contains one non-diatonic note, it really adds a lot of color. Garcia played this lick literally thousands (possibly millions?) of times. He loved those slippery chromatic notes and they will reappear throughout this solo.

In measure 11 we see a scale run—A up to G#—with a G natural snuck in for style. Long scale passages were also a common theme in Garcia's playing. A variation of the same lick happens in measure 14, but this time it starts on a different beat. Garcia was never afraid to play simple, scale-based ideas, though he was always ready to throw in a little rhythmic or chromatic twist.

The solo takes on a completely new feel in measure 16, which features more notes and left-hand articulation. The phrasing in this section uses ideas Garcia explored on *Blues for Allah*, which is by far the Dead's most jazz-inspired album. Pay attention to the unusual combination of hammer-ons, pull-offs, and slides. It would be easy to play these phrases by picking every note, but the various slurs are what give it character.

Starting in measure 24, the next section contains variations on a simple five-note pattern that's filled with tricky triplets. I even put a "mistake" note in there—another Garcia trait. This is a common Garcia lick in which he lets the fingers take over and almost flail about with a sort of reckless precision that's difficult to recreate note-for-note.

There are other key aspects of Garcia's playing that really set him apart from so many guitarists. He would constantly tweak his tone and volume knobs during a solo, move his right hand to various positions to exact a certain timbre, pick alternately hard and soft, and give every note longer than an eighth-note some vibrato. Also pay attention to the long, sustained notes, like those in measures 13, 15, and 31. In true Garcia fashion, these longer notes let the solo breathe.

As I mentioned in the introduction, it can be challenging to know where to start with Garcia. In addition to the Grateful Dead, his work with the Jerry Garcia Band (both electric and acoustic), duo CDs with mandolinist David Grisman, his guest spots on other artist's records, and his solo recordings are all worth checking out. But if pressed to recommend one key recording, I'd have to go with *Live/Dead*. So dive in, pick and choose, take what you want and leave the rest. As Garcia said many times, "My responsibility to the notes is over after I've played them. At that point I don't care where they go."

## Example 10

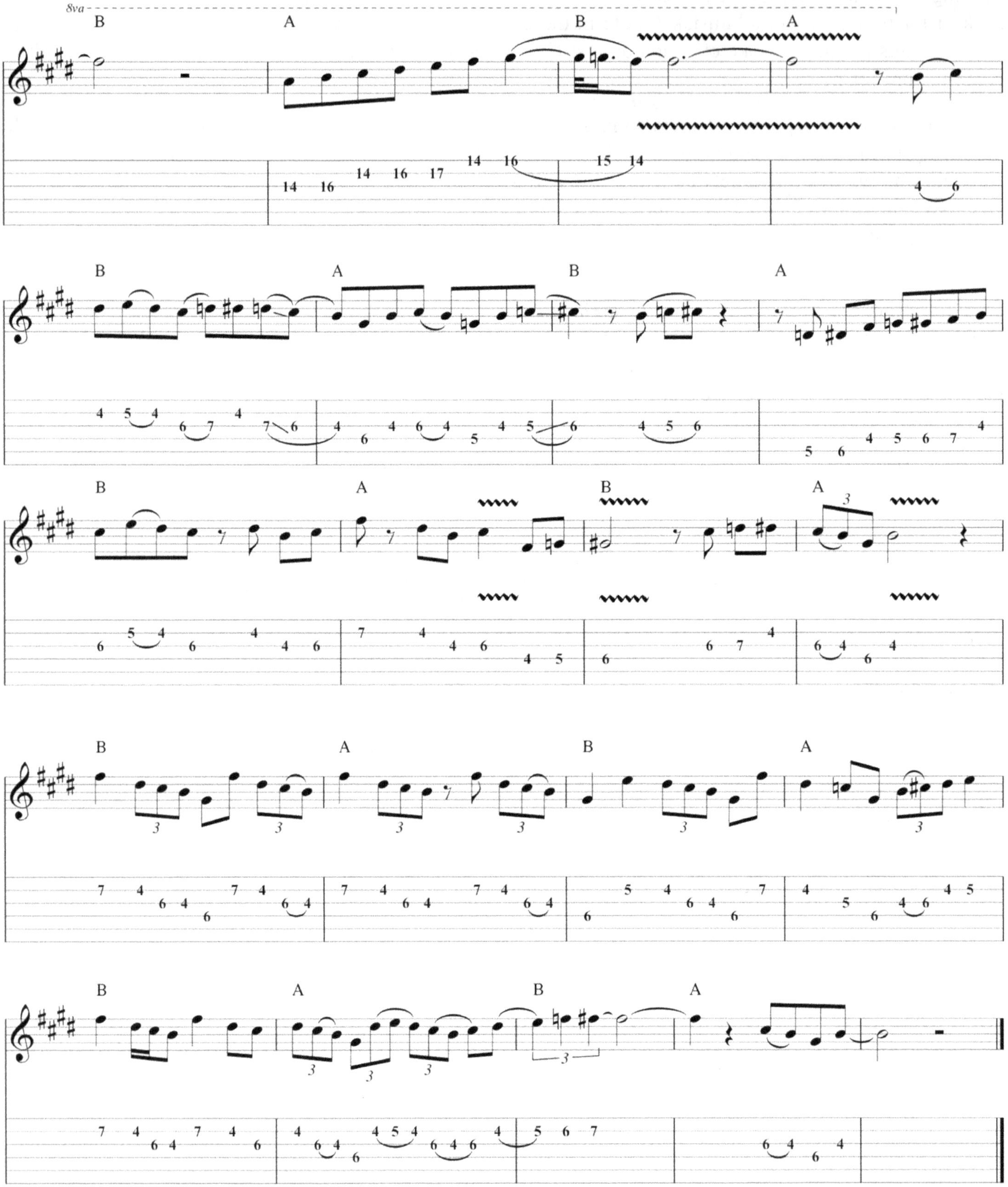
8va
B A B A
B A B A
B A B A
B A B A
B A B A

# Chapter 11: Jerry Cantrell

## By Jamie Humphries

During the late '80s and early '90s, the focus of the music industry shifted towards Seattle and the grunge movement. Gone were the big-hair bands, their spandex and pointy-headstock guitars swept away by groups offering a more blue-collar approach to rock. One of the biggest bands to emerge out of this scene was Alice in Chains. Formed by guitarist Jerry Cantrell, vocalist Layne Staley, drummer Sean Kinney, and bassist Mike Starr, the group had a different sound from other alt-rock bands that emerged from the Emerald City. AIC was much heavier, yet also featured rich vocal harmonies, and even folk and acoustic elements.

Their debut album, *Facelift*, spawned "Man in a Box," which was in heavy rotation on MTV. *Dirt*, the band's multi-platinum second album, proved to be their most successful with "Would?" gaining traction on the soundtrack to the movie *Singles*. Sadly, Staley and Starr (who left the band in 1993 and was replaced by Mike Inez) died from drug-related incidents. In 2006, William Duvall stepped in as vocalist and contributed to the two recent albums, *Black Gives Way to Blue* and *The Devil Put Dinosaurs Here*.

Jerry Cantrell has a very thick and powerful guitar sound that packs plenty of crunch. He's a huge fan of drop-D tuning and likes to layer guitar parts with a variety of tones. For our lesson, I was inspired by both old and new AIC, including "Man in a Box," "Them Bones," "Grind," and "Check My Brain." In this example, I've included droning bends, chugging dropped-tuned riffs, and some melodic chord sequences.

The intro kicks off with a riff inspired by "Check My Brain." You'll notice we're in drop-D tuning, so don't forget to lower your 6th string a whole-step. The riff is based around a bending figure that needs a bit of explanation. Throughout the measure, continue to pick eighth-notes while slowly bending the string up a whole-step. It creates an awesome droning effect and serves as a "question" to the next measure's "answer." You can see we have two alternating answer measures. The first one moves between the open 6th string and C on the 5th string. The alternate measure features a sliding octave shape. To fully emulate the AIC sound, I've doubled this riff an octave higher.

In the next section, we start with a thick rhythm part. For the double-stops, use all downstrokes and keep the chugging feel going. Dig into the strings and drive *through* the riff. Check out the Dm7 voicing at the 10th fret and add some vibrato.

For the chorus, we explore a slightly more open feel that includes some syncopation. This section was inspired by "Grind" from AIC's self-titled album. Focus on connecting the sound between the double-stops and then move to the chugging feel for the Eb5 chords.

Next we move to a 6/4 time signature for the bridge, much like "Them Bones." AIC often favors unusual time signatures, such as 7/8. Here, we keep a similar feel going with some chromaticism as we climb up the neck.

Cantrell is heavily inspired by Jimi Hendrix, and I've tried to capture that in the solo. Things kick off with a fast trill before moving into the D blues scale (D–F–G–Ab–A–C). Pay attention to the huge (minor third) bend in the solo's third measure. Keep it in tune! After a flourish of triplets, we move up to the safe confines of the D minor pentatonic scale (D–F–G–A–C) in the 10th position. After the whole-step bend up to A on the 3rd string, keep it in place while picking the triplets—a classic blues-rock move. In the solo's conclusion, a bit of shred pops up with a fast sextuplet lick based around legato phrasing within the D minor pentatonic scale.

Cantrell is known for his signature G&L Rampage, a guitar he's been using throughout his career. He's also been seen playing Gibson Les Pauls and older Music Man models. Lately, Cantrell's backline consists of Friedman heads (including his signature model) and Bogner cabs.

**Recording details.** For our track, I used my Music Man Axis into JamUp Pro on an iPad, and that was routed to Steinberg's Cubasis via Audiobus. For the crunchy rhythm guitars, I used an amp model based on an old Peavey 5150. To record the solo, I moved to a 5150 MKIII with a model of an MXR Micro Amp in front. Though I didn't use many effects, I added some ambient reverb on the rhythm parts and a stereo delay on the leads. I grabbed a Sterling by Music Man StingRay 5 for the bass parts and ran it through an Ampeg-style amp in JamUp.

## Example 11

Dm7 A5 G5 F5 G5 E♭5 A5 G5 F5 G5 Dm11
D5 A5 G5 F5 G5 E♭5
D5 E5 F5 D5 F5 F♯5 D5 F♯5 G5 D5 G5 G♯5 D5 E5 F5 D5 F5 F♯5 D5 F♯5 G5 D5 G5 G♯5
tr
1 1/2
1/2
T
A
B

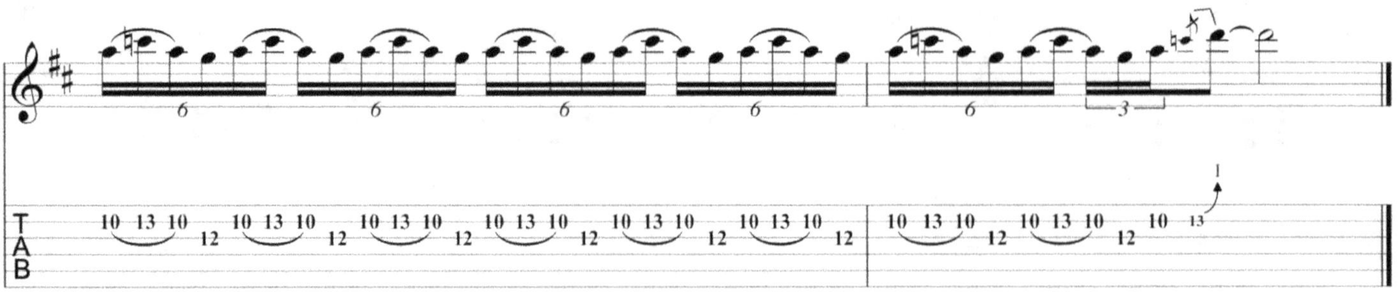

# Chapter 12: Ty Tabor

## By Jamie Humphries

Throughout rock history there have been many genre-defining power trios. For example, the Jimi Hendrix Experience, the Police, Rush, and Cream each created a unique and singular sound. The Texas-based trio King's X helped shape the sound of hard rock by blending crushing altered-tuned riffs with soulful vocals, funky grooves, and Beatles-inspired psychedelic sounds. The trio of bassist Doug "dUg" Pinnick, guitarist Ty Tabor, and drummer Jerry Gaskill are all about groove and melody.

Hailing from Mississippi, Ty Tabor began playing guitar in his early teens, and was influenced by the Beatles, Alice Cooper, Brian May, and Phil Keaggy. His early musical experiences were playing and touring in his father's bluegrass band. After Tabor joined up with Pinnick and Gaskill, the band relocated to Texas and met Sam Taylor, who later became their manager and producer.

In 1989 the band released their landmark album, *Gretchen Goes to Nebraska*, which contained such classic King's X tracks as "Summerland," "The Burning Down," "Over My Head," and the epic "Pleiades." It was a turning point for the band, and the album's success offered King's X the opportunity to embark on large-scale arena support tours with such acts as AC/DC.

King's X continues to tour regularly and release amazing albums. Each member also enjoys a successful solo career, and is involved in side projects with members of Dream Theater, Pearl Jam, and the Dixie Dregs.

Ty Tabor is an incomparable guitarist. He uses a variety of altered tunings, including the grunge-approved dropped-D and a custom dropped-B setup. Tabor's approach to chord arpeggios emphasizes common tones, and he also makes great use of single-coil pickups in a hard rock setting.

King's X is my favorite band of all time, and because Tabor has possibly had more impact on my playing than any other guitarist, this track was a joy to compose. I've focused on isolating elements of "Pleiades," "It's Love," "Summerland," "Over My Head," "Faith Hope Love," and "Dogman" for this lesson. Also, this whole piece is in dropped-D tuning, so make sure to tune that low 6th string down a whole-step.

The track kicks off with an eight-measure verse progression that perfectly illustrates Tabor's approach to arpeggios supported by a moving bass line. This results in a series of slash chords, based around the initial D5 chord. In the last few measures of this section, a three-against-four riff combines two open strings with an ascending line on the 5th string.

I pay tribute to ideas from "It's Love," "Faith Hope Love," and "Dogman" in the next eight-measure section. The first two measures combine some sliding power chords over a syncopated open 5th string. We then move on to some grinding dropped-D chords before repeating the first two measures. Finally, this section ends with an ascending arpeggiated passage that sets up both the repeat and the variation that comes up next.

A double-time feel kicks in during the next four-measure riff. This is based around ideas drawn from "Over My Head" and uses a similar pattern of power chords against an open string. The twist comes during the last measure before the solo with a unison line that's played with the bass ahead of the Bbm7 chord stabs.

The ripping solo combines Hendrix-style bends and double-stops with some over-the-top shredding. We begin with double-stops based around the D minor pentatonic (D–F–G–A–C) and D Dorian (D–E–F–G–A–B–C) scales. In the sixth measure of the solo, I pre-bend the C before launching into a furious legato passage. The trick here is to break it up into smaller pieces and play with a metronome. Take each group of slurred notes and work them out before connecting them.

Tabor's original rig included an early-'80s Fender Elite Strat that featured a mid-boost circuit. His amps of choice were Gibson Lab Series, which were rackmounted and used only as a preamp. Those then ran into a Mesa/Boogie power amp. Currently, Tabor usually favors a Fractal Audio Systems Axe-FX running into a Randall RT2/50 power amp. For pedals, he uses a Line 6 DL4 and a Seymour Duncan Pickup Booster.

**Recording details.** This track was recorded entirely using Cubasis, Steinberg's iPad sequencer and recording software. For guitar and bass tones I used JamUp Pro with an Alesis iO Dock interface. I plugged in my Ernie Ball Music Man Axis Super Sport (on a single-coil setting), and then dialed up a Marshall JCM sound for the rhythm parts and a Mesa/Boogie sound for lead. On the solo, I added a touch of chorus and delay, and for the cleaner tones I simply backed down my guitar's volume knob. The "acoustic" guitars on the backing track were produced with the piezo pickup on the Axis.

## Example 12

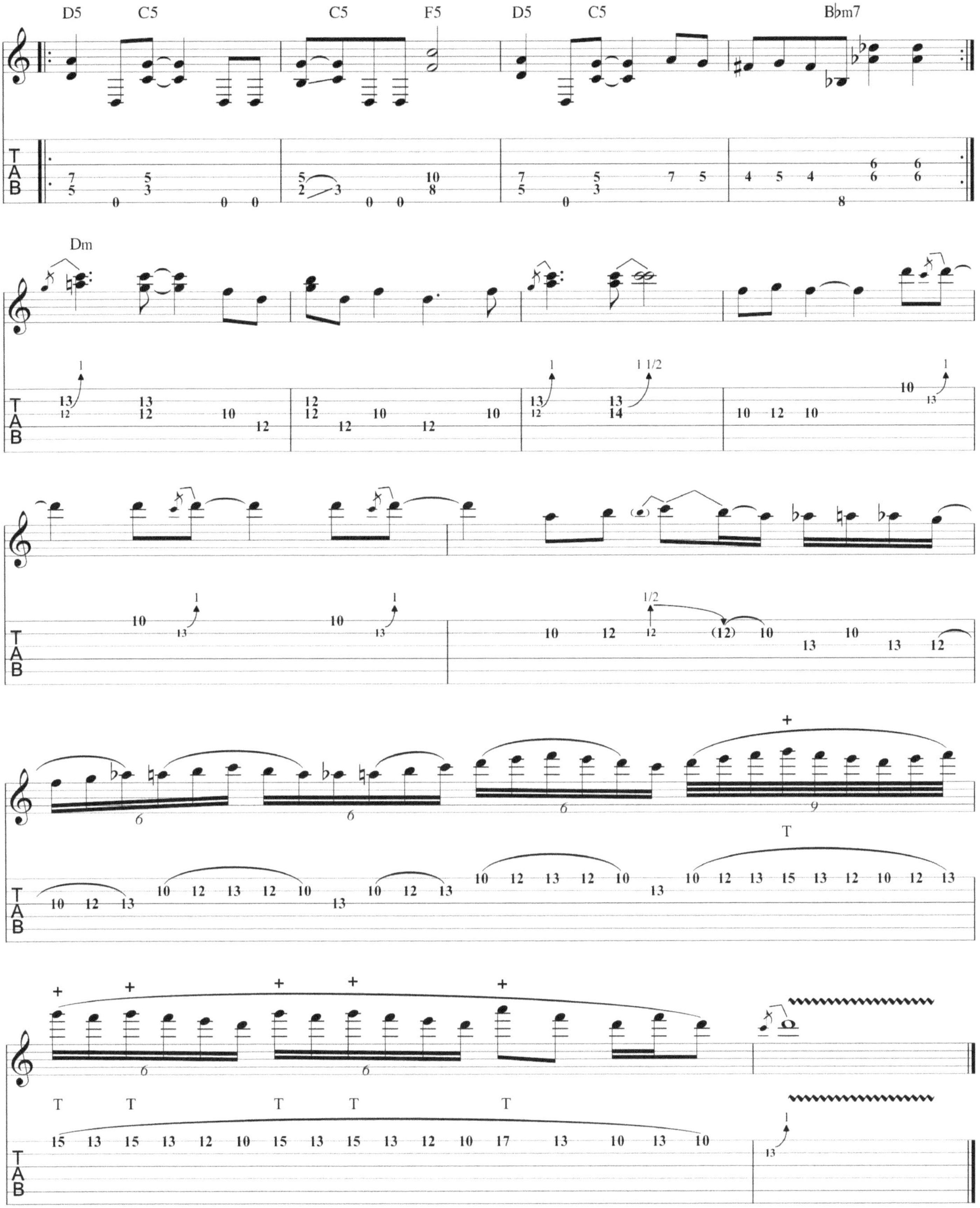
D5
C5
C5
F5
D5
C5
B♭m7
Dm

# Chapter 13: "Dimebag" Darrell

## By Jamie Humphries

If there were ever a band and guitarist to credit for reinventing post-Metallica metal, it would have to be Pantera and the late "Dimebag" Darrell. Pantera pushed the boundaries musically and technically with their unique brand of aggressive power metal.

Born Darrell Lance Abbott in Texas, the guitar slinger started playing at age 12. He began by emulating—both in style and looks—his biggest influence, Kiss' Ace Frehley. Other musical influences, such as Eddie Van Halen and Tony Iommi, worked their way into Abbott's style, and soon he was winning nearly every local guitar competition. On one of those occasions he won a Dean ML, which became a lifelong companion.

In 1981 he formed Pantera with his brother Vinnie Paul on drums and bassist Rex Brown. The original lineup was a spandex-wearing glam metal band, but they soon changed their image and direction when they parted company with the original singer Terry Glaze and instead teamed up with the more vocally aggressive Phil Anselmo.

Pantera went on to become one of the biggest selling metal bands of the '90s, releasing such classic metal albums as *Cowboys from Hell*, *Vulgar Display of Power*, and *Far Beyond Driven*.

Eventually, due to Anselmo's substance use and various members embarking on side projects, the band decided to take a break. Sadly they never played together again. Dime and his brother Vinnie went on to form Damageplan, but tragically Dime was shot and killed onstage during a performance in Columbus, Ohio, in December 2004.

To this day, Dimebag remains one of the most influential and genre-defining guitarists to emerge on the metal scene. He fused aggressive, drop-tuned riffs with blues-based licks reminiscent of Billy Gibbons and fast legato lines that paid homage to Van Halen. Listen to any of his solos and chances are you'll hear some squealing, over-the-top harmonics. Dime would often flip his whammy bar around and push down on it to really make those harmonics pop.

For our track, I've mainly used "I'm Broken" from the *Far Beyond Driven* album for inspiration, although there are also ideas from "Walk" and "Regular People" from *Vulgar* and "Cemetery Gates" from *Cowboys*. Note: Before we start exploring the track, you'll need to drop your 6th string down a whole-step from E to D.

We kick things off with an intro riff based around some bluesy fills using the D minor pentatonic scale (D-F-G-A-C). These licks are broken up with a tight, chugging open 6th string. Keep your picking hand relaxed and pay attention to the 16th-notes. The riff concludes with a syncopated Eb5 chord that requires muting to keep things punchy.

In the ninth measure, our second riff appears ... and it's tricky. Although the riff is predominantly based around a D5 power chord, again it's very tight and makes use of syncopated rhythmic ideas that cross over the barline. The riff is a three-measure figure; the fourth measure features a short D blues scale (D-F-G-Ab-A-C) phrase. The riff repeats twice with the final lick being slightly different each time. This entire sequence repeats, so really pay attention to locking in with bass and drums. And give those rests their full due!

The third riff, which is based around an F diminished interval (F-B), features some tight machine-like 16th-note rhythms. Again, make sure to sonically contrast the chords and tight rhythm parts, and keep your picking hand completely relaxed.

The solo starts with some bluesy wah-fueled bends based around the D minor pentatonic scale. This section concludes with an inverted tritone that shifts up the neck in minor thirds, creating a diminished tonality. Pay attention to the violent whammy vibrato at the end of the phrase.

Next is a classic Dime-style lick that pays homage to Van Halen. This is based around the D blues scale and is very fast, so take your time with the sextuplets. Push the wah pedal down gradually through the lick to add tension and excitement.

Dimebag wasn't afraid to mix and match sounds and tonalities. The next phrase is roughly based in D minor pentatonic with nods to Mixolydian (with the F#) and Dorian. To execute the right-hand tapping in the next section, simply hit the 3rd string on the 7th fret and then slide up that string towards your pickups.

Our final section kicks off with more searing bends. When performing this bend, also catch the 2nd string to add to the sonic intensity. This section concludes with another sextuplet figure, based around a major/minor hybrid lick and a blues scale lick. The cool thing about this? It's the same shape simply shifted up a minor third.

The solo concludes with a high-register bend, followed by a squealing natural harmonic played on the 3rd string at the 3rd fret. When performing this harmonic, start off by scooping into the harmonic with the bar and then raise it as high as your bar will allow, then finish off by lowering the bar. It's worth mentioning that Dime would generate his harmonics by slapping his fretting-hand fingers on the strings to make the harmonics sound.

As I mentioned earlier, Dime was a long-time user of Dean guitars, mainly the ML. Although there was a brief period with Washburn, he later returned to Dean. He'd normally plug into solid-state Randall heads, but also used Krank tube amps. Dime's signal chain would be very simple—just his signature Dunlop wah, an MXR EQ, and a Dime MXR distortion. The delay and noise gate would typically be housed in his rack.

**Recording details.** I used a new Music Man John Petrucci Majesty guitar running straight into a Blackstar ID:60 digital head. For the solo, I used an Ernie Ball wah pedal and added two different delays. One of the delays was a tight stereo delay to give a doubled sound and then I added a longer delay for ambience. I aimed for a scooped sound, pulling out the mids and boosting the bass and treble frequencies. Remember, when using a lot of gain you might benefit from a noise gate, such as an MXR Smart Gate.

## Example 13

Tune ⑥ to D

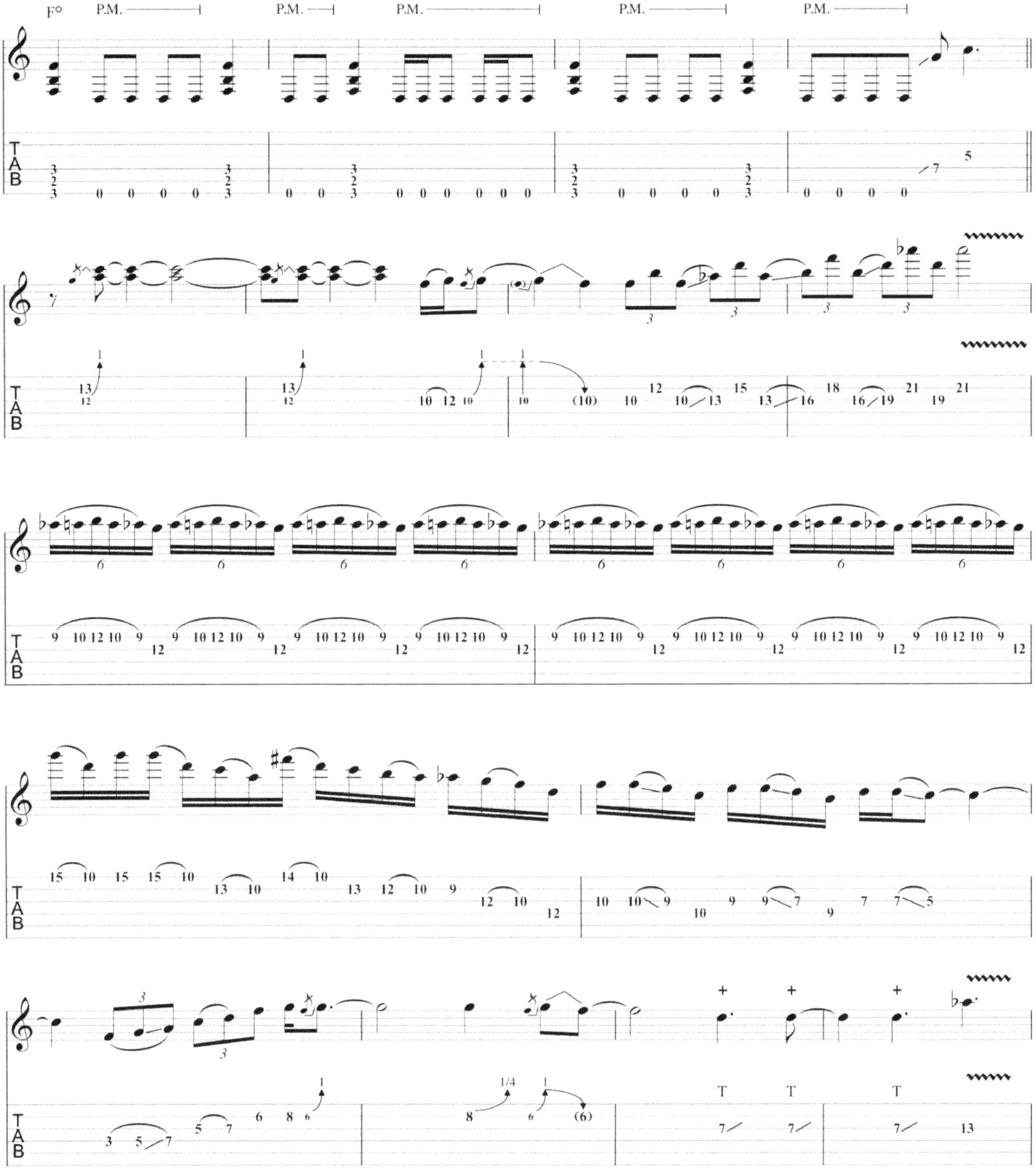
F°
P.M.
P.M.
P.M.
P.M.
P.M.
T
A
B
T
T
T

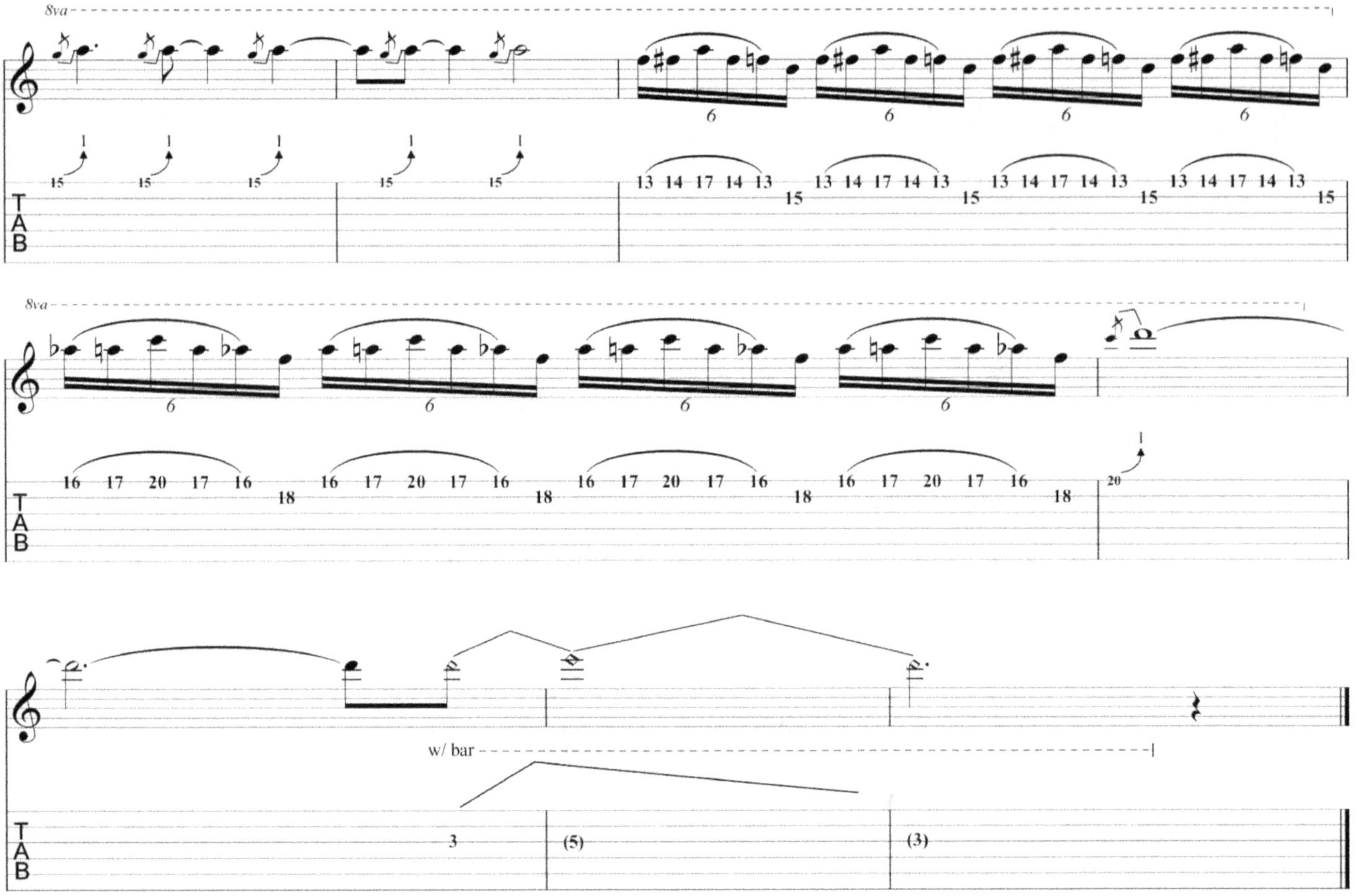
8va
8va
w/ bar

# Chapter 14: Jason Becker

## By Jamie Humphries

Next, we're looking at the legendary shred guitarist Jason Becker. Hailing from Richmond, California, Becker began playing guitar at the age of five, inspired by his father and uncle, who both played guitar. Becker began by learning Bob Dylan songs on his acoustic and performing them for his friends at school. Soon he moved to electric guitar and after watching *The Last Waltz*, he began learning Eric Clapton solos note-for-note. It wasn't long before Becker was diving into Van Halen, Uli Jon Roth, Yngwie Malmsteen—and even Bach and Mozart.

By the time he was 14, Becker was a virtuoso who blended hard rock and heavy metal with classical-inspired harmony and compositions. His father secured him a slot performing at a coffeehouse, and there Becker developed a one-man show. Between his blistering solo guitar performances and stage theatrics, he earned a reputation as a teenage protégé.

At the time, Mike Varney, the head of Shrapnel Records, was looking for talented, unknown guitarists to be featured on his label, so Becker submitted a demo. Varney was floored, not just by Becker's technique, but his rich, deep knowledge of composition, harmony, and counterpoint. Varney offered Becker a deal with Shrapnel, pairing him up with Marty Friedman to form the speed metal band Cacophony. Becker cut his first Cacophony record for Shrapnel, *Speed Metal Symphony*, when he was just 16.

It wasn't long before word of Becker's abilities began to spread, and he joined David Lee Roth's band for *A Little Ain't Enough*. Around the time of the recording, Becker started walking with a limp. He eventually went for tests and was given the devastating news that he had amyotrophic lateral sclerosis, which is sometimes called "Lou Gehrig's Disease." Before the disease totally robbed him of the ability to play, Jason spent time recording, but eventually he was unable to continue as a guitarist. Becker's story may seem tragic, but it's also an inspiring testament to the human spirit and Becker's love of music. To celebrate his amazing life, a full-length movie documentary, *Jason Becker: Not Dead Yet*, was released in 2012 to critical acclaim.

Becker's playing style includes fast alternate picking, sweep picking, legato, tapping, hybrid picking, advanced whammy bar phrasing, and an instantly recognizable vibrato. He often employed a technique of landing on a note that was outside the scale—essentially a "wrong" note—and then slowly bending it to become an inside note. This technique helped with tension and release. Japanese music was also a big influence and Becker was known to employ the Japanese pentatonic scale, or Hirajoshi scale, which is based on the tuning of a koto.

The track I've composed for this lesson borrows ideas from the Cacophony pieces "Images" and "The Ninja," and also Becker's solo composition "Altitudes." As well as having the full track with all of the guitar parts, I've included two backing tracks. The first backing track includes Guitar 2 and Guitar 3 harmony parts, which accompany the composed solo for Guitar 1. The second track has no harmony guitars, and includes only the rhythm guitar, so you can try ideas of your own and don't have to stick with what I've written.

The track kicks off with a very melodic, clean-toned solo based around the B Aeolian (B–C#–D–E–F#–G–A) mode with a first inversion Bm arpeggio. It then moves into one of Becker's signature bending ideas by moving from C# to D. In measure five, we move to a series of sweep-picked Em arpeggios. This demonstrates one the slightly unusual ways that Becker linked shapes—check out the stretch from the 9th to the 4th fret!

Measures seven and eight move to F# and illustrate how Becker might incorporate the F# Phrygian dominant (F#–G–A#–B–C#–D–E) scale over a V–Im resolution. Over this section we use an A#dim7 arpeggio across all six strings to create an F#7b9 sound, and then traverse up the neck using inversions on the top two strings.

Guitar 2 comes in at measure 12 and harmonizes a descending A arpeggio on the top two strings before moving to a D arpeggio across all five strings. This section concludes with a sequence based around one version of the B Hirajoshi (B–C#–D–F#–G) scale. I kick on the distortion in measure 15 for a series of harmonized diminished 7 arpeggios that imply a strong Phrygian dominant sound. The arpeggios are grouped into quintuplets and I use some sweep picking while moving up the neck in minor third intervals. The harmony part for Guitar 2 is the same line, but transposed up a minor third.

Our melodic theme comes in at measure 17 and expands to three different guitar parts with Guitar 1 and Guitar 2 playing in octaves while Guitar 3 adds the harmony. This melody emulates some of the interplay heard between Becker and Marty Friedman, and includes legato phrasing with wide stretches and more outside-to-inside bending ideas. Guitar 1 takes over in measure 23 with a B minor pentatonic (B–D–E–F#–A) phrase that has an angular sound due to some string skipping. I conclude with a diatonic sliding figure that ascends the top two strings.

The next section emulates Becker's flawless sweep-picking technique and shows how he would link five-string arpeggio shapes. We stick with G and F# arpeggios, while moving to a Bm arpeggio near the end of the section. Finally, we finish the example with a sextuplet-based, B Aeolian-infused line and conclude with some harmony squeals.

**Recording details.** To emulate Becker's tone, I used a Music Man Silhouette Special fitted with DiMarzio Area series single-coils in the middle and neck, and a Fast Track Hot Rail in the bridge. Becker's clean tone sounded like a straight DI, so I plugged my guitar directly into my Avalon mic preamp and used the middle and neck single-coils. For the distorted tone, I used a Blackstar Series One 50-watt head feeding an isolation cab equipped with a Shure SM57 mic. This ran into an Avalon valve mic preamp, EQ, and compressor. I also used a Pro Tone signature Jason Becker Distortion pedal, which really delivers his crisp, crunchy tone. Becker's tone had exaggerated high-end EQ that helped the lead guitar sit within the mix. I also added a healthy dose of stereo delay during the mixing process.

# Example 14

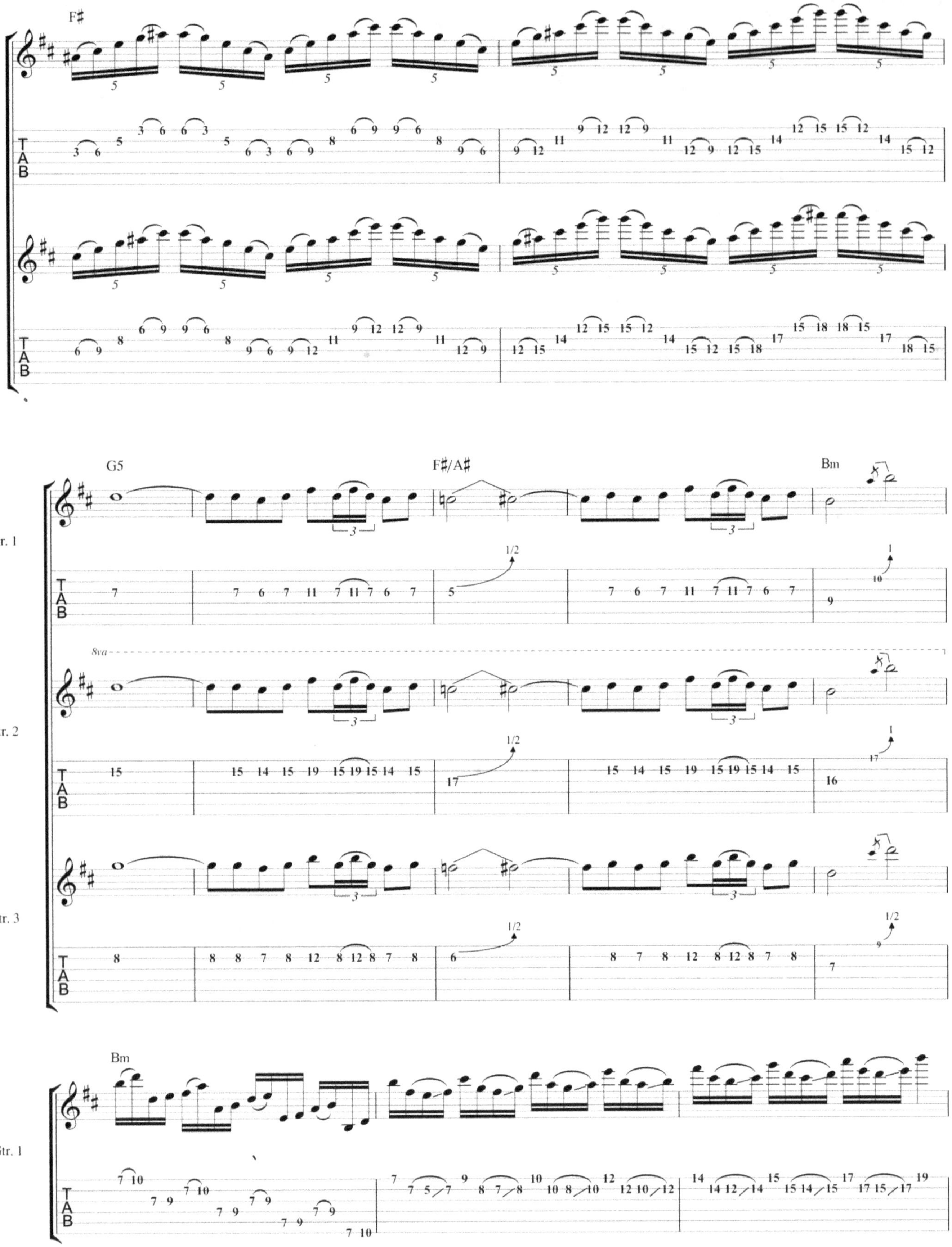
F♯
G5
F♯/A♯
Bm
Gtr. 1
8va
Gtr. 2
Gtr. 3
Bm
Gtr. 1

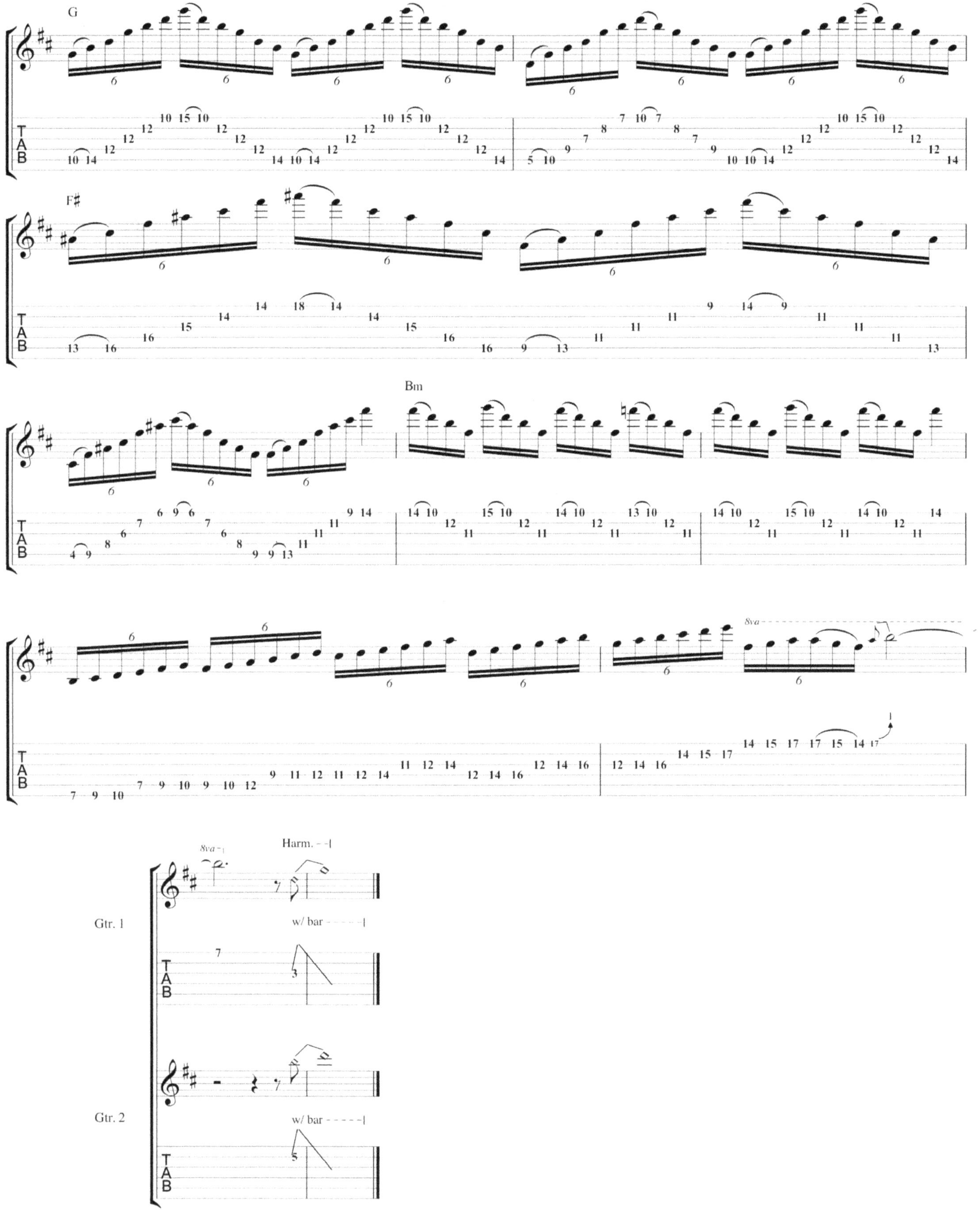
G
F♯
Bm
8va
Harm.
w/ bar
Gtr. 1
Gtr. 2

# Chapter 15: Eddie Van Halen

## By Jamie Humphries

If Jimi Hendrix was the most influential rock guitarist of the late '60s, then Edward Van Halen is without a doubt the most important rock guitarist to emerge during the latter part of the '70s. After relocating to California from the Netherlands, Van Halen completely reinvented modern rock guitar and totally changed everything that came after him. Along with his brother Alex on drums, bassist Michael Anthony, and manic frontman David Lee Roth, Van Halen would go on to spearhead one of the biggest rock bands of all time. The group's catchy, hook-filled songs scored high on the charts and were the perfect vehicle for Eddie's blistering guitar work.

For this chapter I've focused on the sound of vintage Van Halen tracks like "I'm the One" and "Hot for Teacher." The licks in the solo can be heard in numerous Van Halen songs and will give you a pretty good overview of his style. The main challenge will be the feel of the rhythm part. It's an up-tempo shuffle that clocks in at a death-defying 230 bpm. The tendency will be to play the eighth-notes with a straight feel, but try to swing them as much as you can. I've tried to include as many "Eddie-isms" as possible in this track.

The opening riff kicks things into high gear and is inspired by the groove from "I'm the One." It's built around an open-string figure based on the 5th string, and includes a speedy triplet move on the 4th string. The double-stops in both the first and second endings give a nod to Eddie's fretwork in "Hot for Teacher."

Eddie loves to use natural harmonics and I've included a bunch in the next section. These are fairly simple to play, but the key is developing just the right touch to make them pop. Place one of your fretting-hand fingers (usually your middle finger) directly over the fret shown in the tab. Don't fret the note, but place just enough pressure to sound the harmonic when you pluck the string. If you're new to this technique, start over the 12th fret—those are the easiest harmonics to generate.

The solo section kicks off with a flowing legato phrase that pops up in several of Van Halen's most famous lead breaks. The lick is quite tricky and mixes up several different rhythms. The opening flurry is played entirely on the 1st string before you descend across the strings and end with a pair of bends.

Harmonics appear again in the next section of the solo. While holding the bend up to C#, tap on the indicated frets to sound the artificial harmonics. These harmonics will be diatonic to the fretted note, namely a third or fifth. Hints of "Eruption" come next with a two-measure phrase that uses tremolo picking to walk up an A Lydian (A–B–C#–D#–E–F#–G#) scale.

Take it easy with the wide legato stretches in the next section. Start them slow and make sure each note comes through clearly before you increase the tempo. At the end of this phrase, I mix up the rhythm again and add in a quintuplet—a rhythmic figure that incorporates five notes in a single beat.

It would be hard to overestimate the importance of right-hand string tapping in Van Halen's technique. He likely wasn't the first one to do it, but he took it to places nobody had ever thought of. As a tribute to the groundbreaking "Eruption," the next section of the solo is a very long legato phrase that screams all things Eddie. I start by arpeggiating an Am triad (A–C–E) before moving to an F triad (F–A–C). Since both triads share two common tones, the shift is as simple as moving the tapped note from the 12th fret to the 13th. More "Eruption" hijinks happen with a legato phrase that's based around the A blues scale (A–C–D–Eb–E–G). With enough gain, these licks should flow pretty smoothly.

**Recording details.** For our track, I used my Music Man Axis Super Sport, a guitar derived from the original EVH Music Man. The guitar tones came from Positive Grid's JamUp Pro for iPad via an Apogee Jam interface. I panned the guitar to the left and added reverb on the right during mixdown. This technique adds space to the mix and is very apparent on Van Halen's first album.

For the solo, I used a little bit more gain with a model of an MXR Micro Amp in JamUp and added both reverb and echo to the right side. Eddie's tone is a lot cleaner than you may think, so don't go for a saturated metal tone. To get that vintage EVH bite, make sure you don't scoop out the midrange. Instead, try to dial out some of the lows and add some top-end presence.

**Example 15**

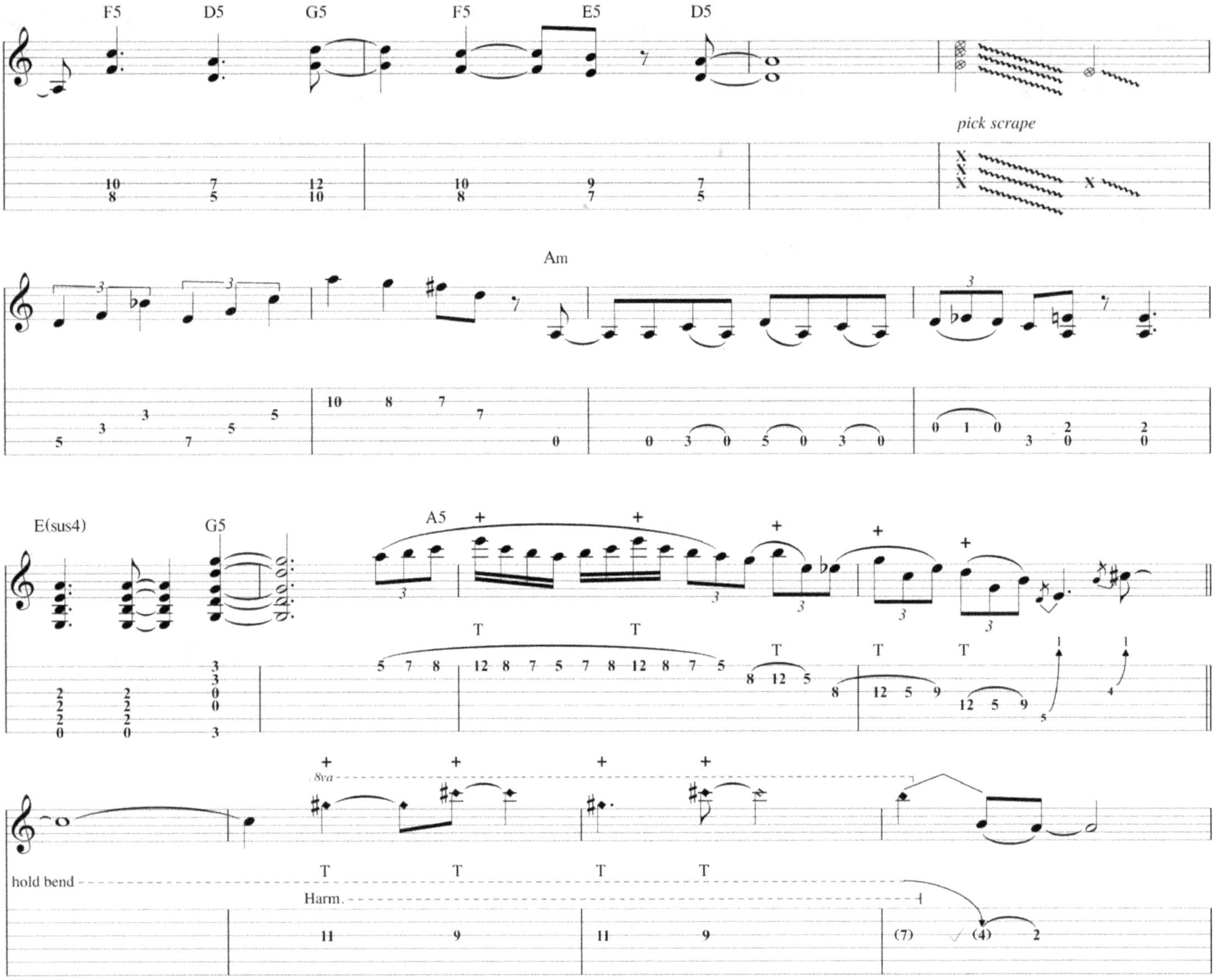
F5
D5
G5
F5
E5
D5
pick scrape
Am
E(sus4)
G5
A5
hold bend
Harm.
8va

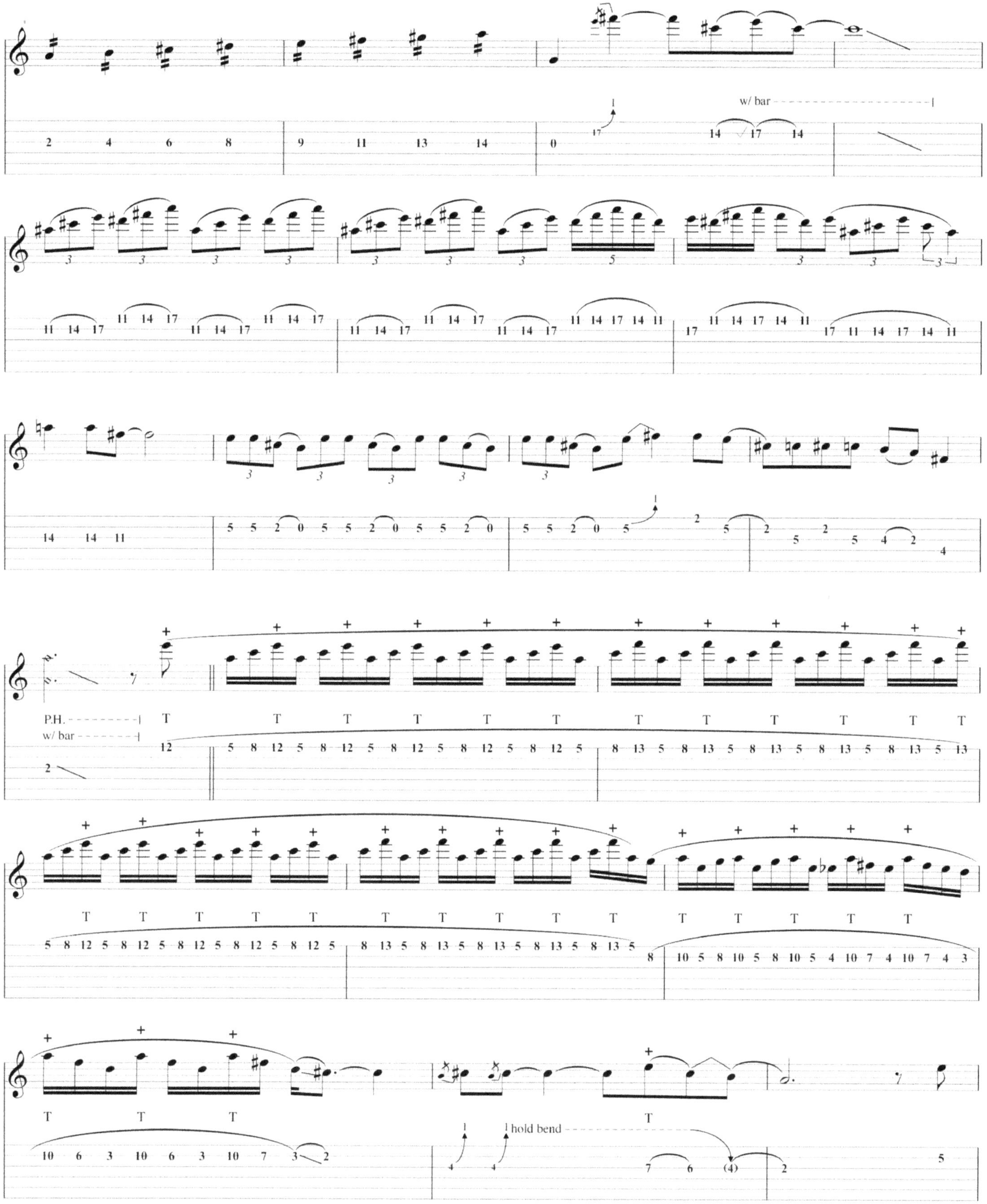
w/ bar
P.H.
w/ bar
hold bend

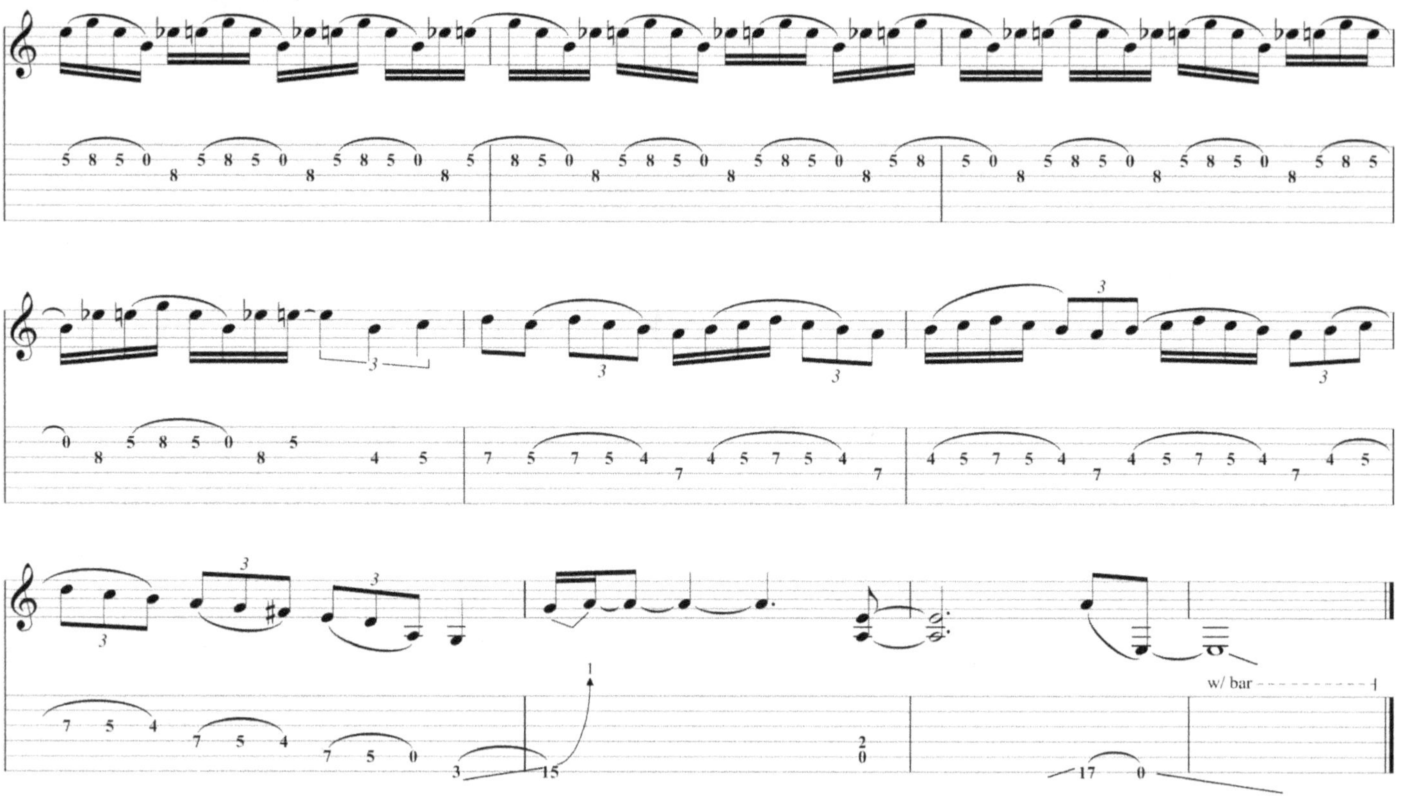
w/ bar

# Chapter 16: Guthrie Govan

## By Sam Bell

Guthrie Govan has the technical and musical abilities that make him one of the most sought-after players in the industry, and he just keeps getting better! Whether rocking out with Dizzee Rascal, writing prog records with Steven Wilson, collaborating on soundtracks with the great Hans Zimmer, or touring with the Aristocrats, Guthrie raises the bar every time he straps on his guitar.

In this lesson, we'll touch a bit on all those styles and delve deep into Guthrie's breakthrough solo album, *Erotic Cakes*. Before releasing *Erotic Cakes* in 2006, he submitted a demo to a guitar magazine and ended up winning a contest. (That demo eventually turned into "Wonderful Slippery Thing.") The attention landed him a position as a music transcriber before he began to tour with Asia in the late 1990s. When not touring, Guthrie would play gigs around town with the Fellowship, a funk/fusion band that still occasionally performs in the U.K. Over the years, Guthrie's riveting YouTube videos have brought him exposure to a wide international audience.

For this lesson, I've gone digital and used Positive Grid's Bias FX for the guitar sounds. The overdriven amps are models of a plexi Marshall with the gain quite high and plenty of midrange, and I've used various room and hall reverbs to create space. For the clean lead moments, I used a tweed Fender model with an MXR-inspired compressor in front of it, enhanced with a bit of studio room reverb. I'm playing a guitar made by Eternal Guitars with two low-output '60s-style single-coils and a PAF-style humbucker in the bridge.

I've written a few unique examples that feature some of what I feel are key elements of the guitar playing on the *Erotic Cakes*, and, of course, Guthrie's own style. Each example has lots of different ideas, approaches, and concepts to take away, play with, and explore further. To develop subtle variations on these core ideas, I'd strongly suggest doing some deeper research into Guthrie's music.

### Slippery Things

One of the tunes on *Erotic Cakes* that guitarists talk most about is "Waves." It first appeared on a compilation album called *Guitar on the Edge* back in the early '90s. The song features a 16th-note motif that works as a main theme throughout the song. Guthrie has said the melody was inspired by the *portamento*, or glide effect, on a keyboard. The melody was quad tracked for an ultra-expansive sound that really does sound like, well, waves.

Upon studying Guthrie's tune, I discovered that the melody highlights arpeggios from the underlying chord progression. The arpeggios feature quite large intervallic jumps, and the use of lots of slides and legato keeps the melody sounding smooth. My melody outlines F#m, B, and A using some linear arpeggio fingerings and sliding sixths (**Example 16a**).

It can be tricky to find one particular fingering that works for everyone. In fact, my choice of fingerings changed several times while writing this lesson. My advice would be to make sure that when you're sliding up on a string, you have a finger behind the one you're sliding with ready to grab the next note. Most of the ascending phrases on one string are often followed by a descending phrase. See if you can find other patterns in the other arpeggios for this progression to use in your own composition and playing. I've found this style of riffing is common in lots of modern tech-metal bands, such as Periphery and Sikth. In **Example 16b**, you can see an isolated instance of one of the arpeggios.

## Example 16a

## Example 16b

## Funk-Bop

Maybe my example song names aren't as creative as Guthrie's, but it's not the easiest job breaking down his exceptionally versatile guitar style into bite-sized chunks! Based on moments from "Wonderful Slippery Thing," **Example 16c** features some of Guthrie's funky rhythm work, slap guitar, and even some jazzy bebop-inspired licks. I've tried my best to demonstrate some key ideas in a few measures. Let's go!

The first measure features a slap guitar riff. It uses a moving octave pattern that travels with the use of the open 6th string in groups of four. (Scott Mishoe is well known for his incredible slap guitar skills, and Guthrie has mentioned his name at many master classes as the inspiration for using this technique.)

A "slap" is when the thumb comes down on the guitar string near the neck, and a "pop" is executed by bringing the strumming hand's index or middle finger under the string and plucking upwards. The pattern starts with a slap on the open string followed by a hammered-on note on the same string, followed by a muted slap, which is executed by muting with the fretting hand and slapping with the fretting hand. The last of the four notes is a pop on the note that's an octave above the second note in the pattern.

The example then breaks into some funky syncopated strumming based around an Em9 chord that moves up a half-step to Fm9. This rhythmic motif continues with the addition of a quick 16th-note-triplet muted strum. The key to getting this sounding smooth and funky is to lighten up on the pick attack for the faster strumming and focus on the strong accents instead.

# Example 16c

**Moderately** ♩ = 104

N.C.

*S = Strike ("slap") string w/ pick-hand thumb.

**P = Snap ("pop") string w/ pick-hand index or middle finger.

Em9

[1.]

Fm9

[2.]

Fm9

Em9

[1.]

Fm9

[2.]

Fm9

The first bebop-inspired phrase of the solo in **Example 16d** outlines notes from the E Dorian mode (E–F#–G–A–B–C#–D) along with some chromatic enclosures. On beat 3 of the second measure, we slip into an Fm7 (F–Ab–C–Eb) arpeggio before heading back to our E minor tonality. Guthrie frequently uses this kind of staggered phrasing with arpeggios to create interest and build upon memorable motifs and themes in his solos.

In the fourth measure, we have a 16th-note-triplet line that highlights notes from the E minor pentatonic scale (E–G–A–B–D) with an added 9 (F#). However, we're including some chromatic enclosures between the scale notes to create a longer, smoother line. Guthrie is known for his relentless picking technique, and I'm quite sure he doesn't think about it too much. He will go between various sequences and picking techniques in one phrase. It's all about the musicality of the line for him, the technique is just there to execute the idea he hears in his head at the time.

Perhaps one of my personal favorite things about Guthrie's playing is his use of slides that seem to add a whole new life to what could be quite a mechanical line. The phrase in the seventh measure uses notes from the E minor pentatonic scale, but in groups of five. The line moves in a reverse linear-style fashion with a slide before the first note of each quintuplet. For this line, I'm picking all the notes, but you can choose your own way of playing it to suit your style.

This final phrase is an ode to how "Wonderful Slippery Thing" finishes, yet not as advanced as Guthrie might play it. This is an E minor pentatonic scale played legato with string skipping and tapping. To build up speed over time, practice slowly and stay relaxed. Once you can handle this phrase, you'll be ready for some of the lines in our next example.

## Example 16d

**Snake Bite**

**Example 16e** references "Hangover," the final track on *Erotic Cakes*. Guthrie wrote the tune to musically express the feeling of being hungover. (I've named my tune after a U.K. drink that's mostly cider topped off with beer.) By mixing a slow tempo with long legato slurs and gravity-defying bends, Guthrie has brilliantly depicted the effects of a hangover with his solo phrasing.

This line that starts in the fifth measure might look terrifying in tab, but try to break it apart into small segments. The first two groups of seven make a slurred blues lick that's great for slipping into any guitar jam. The rest of the phrase plays around a two-octave Bm7 arpeggio (B–D–F#–A). Guthrie does a lot of this with his faster legato lines, as it creates rhythmic interest and gives the phrase a vocal or sax-like dynamic shape. The rhythmic subdivisions shouldn't be followed too closely, just take the underlying pattern and mess around with it. The subdivisions will probably happen naturally due to the line's structure.

More gravity-defying bends start in the 11th measure, this time with a more gospel or blues flavor. The tonality of the backing track has now gone back to Bm and highlights the G and A chords. I'm visualizing B minor pentatonic (B–D–E–F#–A) notes for this phrasing, as well as going for a bluesy sound by adding some slides and slurs to the scale's b5 (F).

The final phrase of this solo is actually a reference to Guthrie's song "Eric," which features an eerie and beautiful melody that uses what I can only describe as pick tapping. Use the pick to tap the higher note and let it bounce off the string for an ultra-fast trill between two notes. This phrase outlines notes from an F#7#5 tonality. In this case, I'm using notes from the F# Phrygian dominant (F#–G–A#–B–C#–D–E) scale over the F# altered chord. The phrase uses a rhythmic motif that moves down through the positions before landing on the 9 (C#) of Bm.

You may notice there are lots of squeaks and pops during this solo. These are deliberately left in to give more of a human vibe to the sound. Guthrie's playing is technically amazing, but it's also very human—it sounds like he is really *playing* the guitar and sometimes these details and sonic artifacts are part of what makes the guitar such an appealing instrument. It's real and it's alive, so enjoy it!

## Example 16e

*Played behind the beat.

## Odd Meter Peter

Guthrie is no stranger to progressive rock, and there are a couple of tunes on *Erotic Cakes* that feature odd time signatures. His tune "Fives" was inspired by a melody he heard a bird singing in a park while on a walk to refresh his creativity. This melody happened to be in 5/4 and the rest is history. There's also a tune on the album called "Sevens." Written in 7/4, it features a cascading tapping arpeggio section that sounds like a piano. I have attempted to create a short piece that pushes 5/4 and 7/4 together with all the traits from both songs. It's named "Odd Meter Peter" after Pete Riley, who played drums on the album.

**Example 16f** starts off in 5/4, which means we have five quarter-notes per measure, or 10 eighth-notes. Before writing the riff, I set out a chord sequence for the riff to follow. The riff uses a mixture of minor 7 and major 7 arpeggios with the addition of some Andy Summers-like add9 arpeggios in measures five and six. To keep this piece interesting, yet accessible for the listener, I employed a bit of repetition with some subtle turnarounds.

In the ninth measure, we move to 7/4 and explore some arpeggio-tapping ideas inspired by the main section of "Sevens." This time we're using a 16th-note subdivision and a "cookie-cutter" approach to the arpeggios that can easily be applied in other contexts. The best way to visualize these patterns is in two-string fragments. First, practice moving between the first two beats. You'll notice that a portion of the measure repeats in beats 3 and 4 before dropping down an octave. This is similar to a section of "Sevens." For the tapping, I'm using my middle and ring fingers. The top string of each phrase is tapped with the ring finger, followed by the middle finger on the string below. In each arpeggio there's a symmetry between the left- and right-hand fingerings that makes this a lot easier to see on the guitar than it is to read from the tab.

As a fan of Guthrie, I know his playing has always inspired me to be more creative and push past my own limitations. I hope this lesson inspires you to do the same.

**Example 16f**

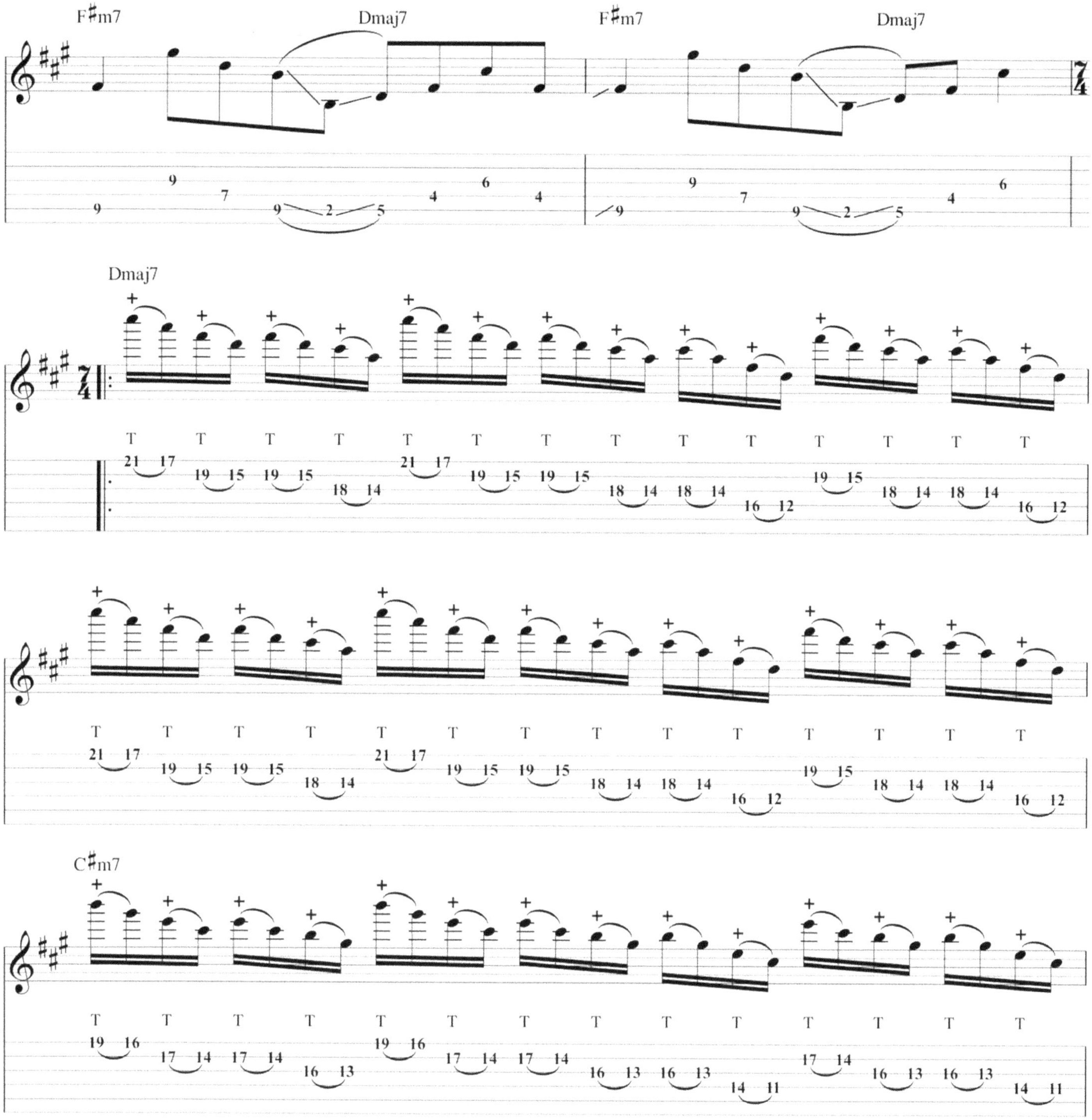
F♯m7
Dmaj7
F♯m7
Dmaj7
Dmaj7
C♯m7

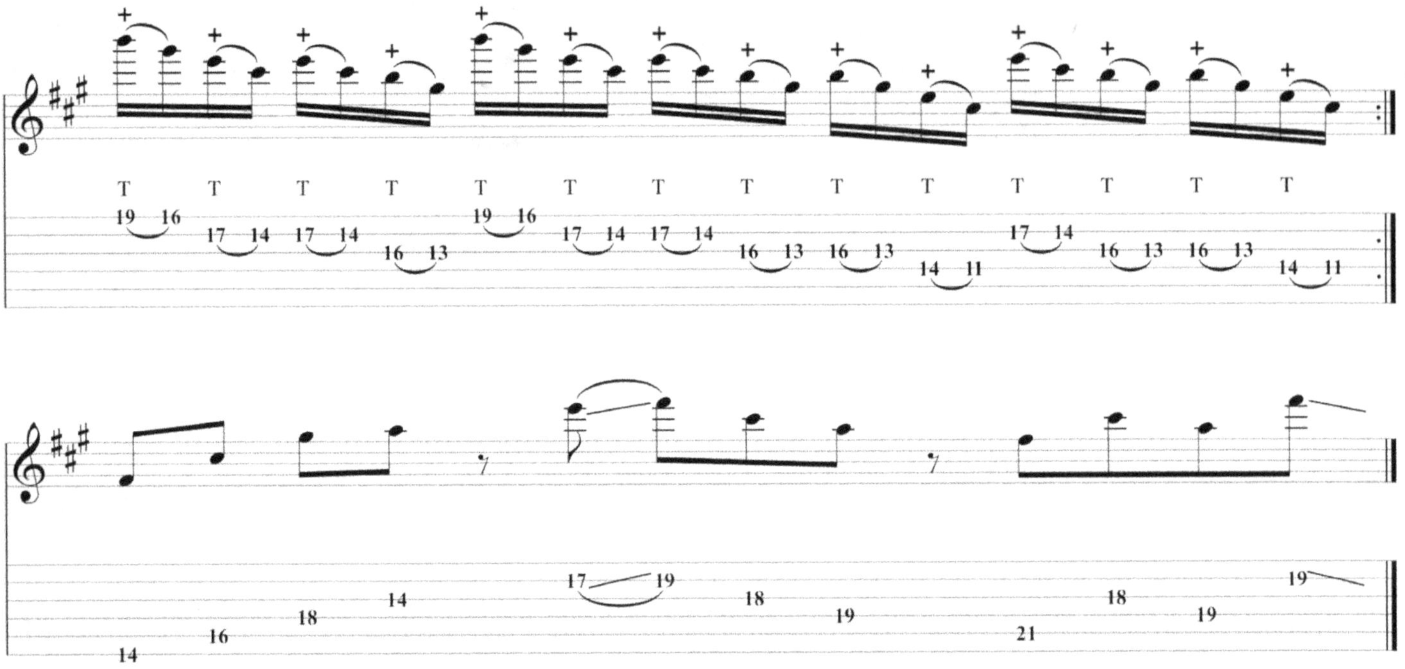

# Chapter 17: Steve Lukather

## By Sam Bell

Released back in 1982, Toto's *IV* album yielded two chart-topping hits, "Africa" and "Rosanna." This remarkable band and album featured a dream lineup centered around guitar legend Steve Lukather. For this lesson, I had the pleasure of breaking down some key aspects of his rhythm and lead playing on *IV* and then working them into my own example, which I've nicknamed "Joanna."

### Get the Tones

I've divided the example track into three main guitar sections: a solo, dirty rhythm, and some clean overdubs. I attempted to get as close to the original sounds on the album as possible using Positive Grid's Bias FX plug-in. For the overdriven sounds, I used an amp based on a Mesa/Boogie Mark IV with a very light slapback delay and a room reverb. All the dirty rhythm examples are double-tracked and panned hard left and right to create a wider stereo sound. For the lead tone, I put an Ibanez TS808 in front of the amp with the drive turned down, but the level slightly boosted to increase sustain. I also added a fairly large hall reverb and a tape-style delay to create ambience. Combined with some chorus, these really expand the lead tone in a classic '80s way. For the clean overdub sounds, I used a basic Twin-style combo with an MXR Dyna Comp in front of the amp, plus a little slapback delay *after* the amp to create space around the part. For the ambient clean sound, I added a large hall reverb and tape echo delay at the end of the signal chain, and then placed a studio-style compressor on the output to let these ambient effects really bloom.

You'll hear that "Joanna" is a homage to "Rosanna," which features drummer Jeff Porcaro's addictive and groovy shuffle. For my example, I used Toontrack's EZdrummer 2, which offers some "Rosanna"-style grooves that I modified. For this groove, we can feel every pair of eighth-notes as a quarter-note and an eighth-note in the space of a single triplet. Describing it makes it sound a lot more complicated than it really is—listening to the track and counting eighth-notes will highlight this time feel in a more intuitive way.

### Luke's Licks

In **Example 17a**, we start off near the end of my track with the main guitar solo. This solo is based over three chords: G for eight measures, Em for four, and finally a Csus2 for the last four. Over the G chord, I'm playing notes from G Lydian (G–A–B–C#–D–E–F#). I start the solo by ascending through a G major triad (G–B–D) before landing on a bend that highlights the 7 (F#) and 9 (A).

Luke is a master of off-kilter triplet runs, so I tried to cop some of that vibe. In measure seven, I start a rather long triplet run that uses chromatic notes and slurs. Pay close attention to the hammer-on and slide markings on the tab to ensure smooth execution of this line. Runs that use chromatic notes are very typical of Lukather's unique playing style. Here, I'm visualizing a Bm7 arpeggio (B–D–F#–A) starting on the 3rd string in 14th position. Since Bm7 is diatonic to G Lydian, it implies a Gmaj9 tonality.

In measure nine, we move to an E minor tonality. This is still diatonic to G Lydian, but now we can open up some E Dorian (E–F#–G–A–B–C#–D) sounds. We start with some expressive bends in bars 11 and 12 that feature another of Steve Lukather's signature moves. There's a tricky bend in measure 11. Use your third finger to bend the B at the 17th fret up a whole-step. While still holding the bend, use your pinky to reach over one fret to add a half-step to the bend. This is a really cool trick for getting gravity-defying bends!

Another triplet phrase pops up in measure 13, but this time I'm thinking of an E blues scale (E–G–A–Bb–B–D) to fill in the gaps. The solo then moves around to a Csus2 tonality, and this time I'm thinking in terms of C major.

## Example 17a

**Example 17b** features two separate parts double-tracked to create a more expansive stereo sound. Guitar 1 has a funky syncopated octave motif starting on the "and" of beat 3 every two measures. This part fills in the space when the ambient clean overdubs and piano take a brief pause on a chord. It's a subtle way to add more groove to the track.

To get a nice, slow attack on this part, I palm-muted the notes on the 6th string while digging in quite hard with a flexible .70 mm celluloid pick. Guitar 2 plays different chords over the A bass note to create a bit of movement over this harmonically static groove—something that can be heard in a lot of Toto's music. I strum each chord quite slowly and softly around the guitar's bridge area to let the chords bloom into the sonic picture. Like all these double-tracked parts, I made sure each side was executed identically, thus adding to the size and depth of the sound.

### Example 17b

Let's move to **Example 17c**, which features double-tracked rhythm guitars over the verse. Notice how big chunky power chords highlight the changes, and how the single-note lines accent the triadic movement of the static groove. When double-tracking these guitars, I chose a slightly less saturated sound for each guitar and focused on keeping the articulations the same on each track. When done right, these double-tracking techniques can make a simple guitar part like this sound huge without getting in the way of the other instruments in the recording.

**Example 17c**

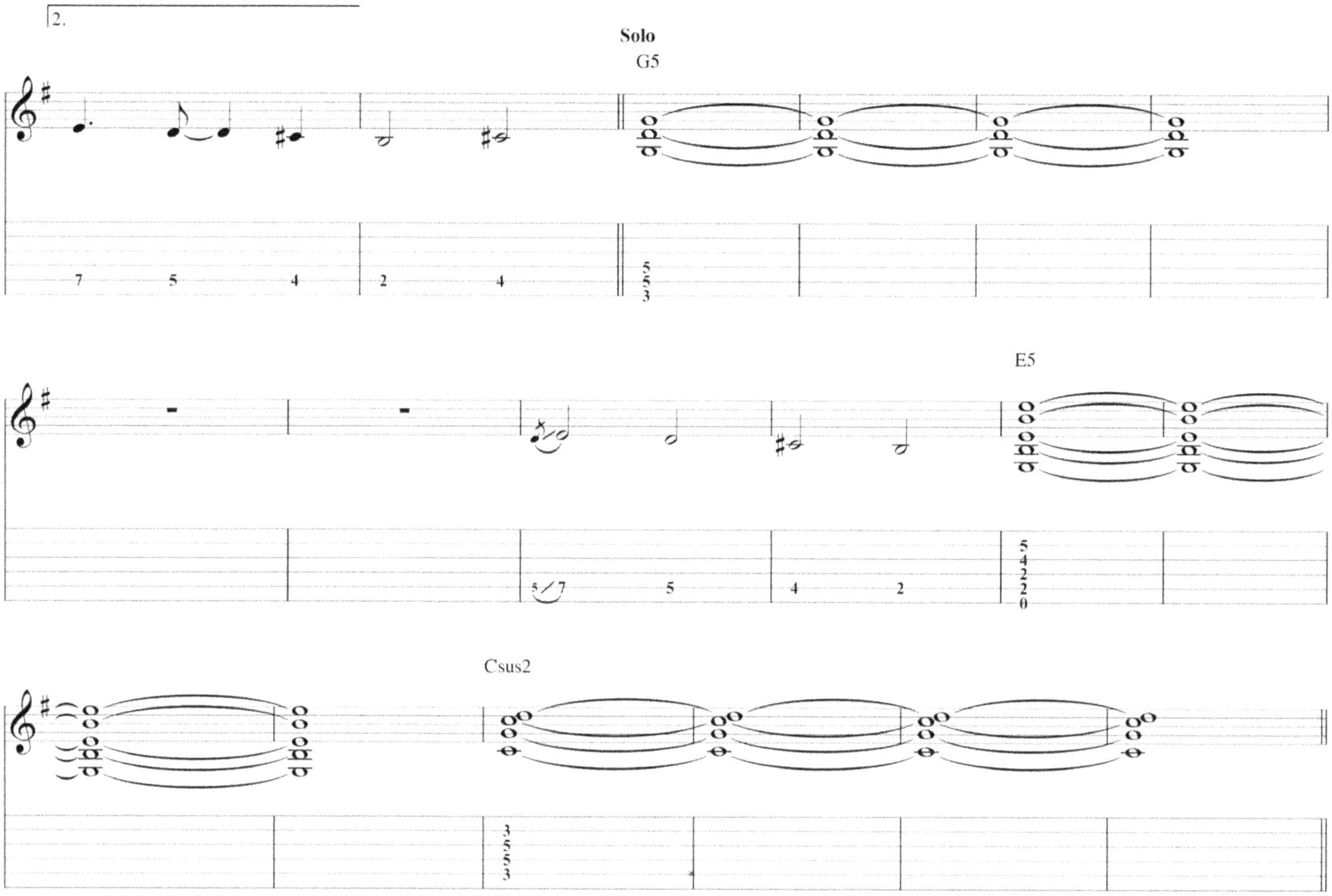
2.
Solo
G5
E5
Csus2

# More from Premier Guitar

See these and more at **shop.premierguitar.com**

*Acoustic DIY Vol.1*

*Acoustic Gigging, Recording & Maintenance Tips Vol.1*

*Acoustic Lessons Vol.1*

*Acoustic Soundboard Vols. 1-3*

*All About Amps Vols. 1-7*

*Best of State of the Stomp Vols. 1-3*

*Beyond Blues Vol. 1*

*Bring the Heavy Vols. 1-3*

*Country Guitar 101*

*DIY Guitar Makeover Vols. 1-2*

*Gig Advice Vol. 1*

*Guitar Shop 101: Acoustic Upkeep Vol. 1*

*John Bohlinger's Last Call Vol. 1*

*Mod Garage: Guitar-God Mods Vol. 1*

*Mod Garage: Stratocaster Mods Vols. 1-2*

*Mod Garage: Telecaster Mods Vol. 1*

*Nothing But Bass Vols. 1-2*

*Pedal Phreakery Vols. 1-3*

*Pedalboards of the Stars Vols. 1-3*

*Pickup Passion Vol. 1*

*Rig Rundown Smash Hits Vols. 1-3*

*Studio Secrets Vols. 1-4*

*Super Strat Mods Vol. 1*

*The Best of Ask Amp Man Vols. 1-2*

*The CAGED System Demystified*

*Tone Tips: Greatest Hits Vols. 1- 2*

*Vintage Vault Gems Vols. 1-2*

*Will Ray's Bottom Feeder Vol. 1*